THE COMMONWEALTH AND INTERNATIONAL LIBRARY

SOCIAL STUDIES
General Editor A. H. RICHMOND

THE SOCIAL STRUCTURE OF MODERN BRITAIN

The Social Structure of Modern Britain

BY

E. A. JOHNS, B.Sc.(Econ.)

Lecturer in Management and Public Administration, Exeter Technical College

PERGAMON PRESS

OXFORD · LONDON · EDINBURGH · NEW YORK
PARIS · FRANKFURT

Pergamon Press Ltd., Headington Hill Hall, Oxford
4 & 5 Fitzroy Square, London W.1
Pergamon Press (Scotland) Ltd., 2 & 3 Teviot Place, Edinburgh 1
Pergamon Press Inc., 122 East 55th Street, New York 10022
Pergamon Press GmbH, Kaiserstrasse 75, Frankfurt-am-Main

First edition 1965
Library of Congress Catalog Card No. 65-25331

Set in 10 *on* 12 *pt Imprint*
and printed in Great Britain by
Billing & Sons Ltd., Guildford and London

(2281/65)

To

Annabel Susan Charlotte
(*born 10 May 1963*)

SOCIAL: 7. Pertaining, relating, or due to, connected with, etc., society as a natural or ordinary condition of human life.

STRUCTURE: 6. An organized body or combination of mutually connected and dependent parts or elements.

From: The Shorter Oxford English Dictionary

Contents

Introduction

THIS book is about society in general and English society in particular. In one single volume it is not possible to give more than a very elementary account of the manifold aspects of our social structure, and it has been necessary to omit entirely some problems—those of urban sociology and of industrial relations, for example—in order to devote sufficient attention to, say, social class and educational selection in this country. Society is like a huge and complicated jigsaw; each of the chapters in this study concerns one or more of the pieces. I hope that when the whole has been joined together some view of contemporary English society will emerge which, if not entirely complete and comprehensive, will at least be an accurate reflection of our social background.

For obvious reasons, each component of society is here treated virtually in isolation, so that separate sections are allocated to political, religious and other facets; but it cannot be too strongly emphasized that in practice none of these elements operates in such isolation. All social processes exert influence over, and in turn are influenced by, other social processes, so that although different sociologists at different times may place very great stress on the ascendency of individual social forces, they can never afford to ignore the countervailing importance of sociological pressures as a whole. To this extent, the chapter divisions which follow represent an artificially contrived breakdown of the social structure, but I must plead (in mitigation) that without some such system of classification it would not be possible to study society at all. In addition, everyday observation suggests that there is some justification for referring to specifically economic, political, educational and other categories as a basis for further inquiry. These descriptive divisions, of course, have no objective reality of their own: just because the class structure has a persistence beyond the lives of particular individuals, this does not mean that it is a real entity in itself, for its perpetuation depends solely on the actions and attitudes of its constituent parts. British sociology has an empirical tradition which lends itself easily to the study of social structure, that is, the way in which the broad pattern of the community exhibits regularities and organization, whether formal or informal. If society is a jigsaw, it is the task of this book to determine the shape of the pieces and then to examine the content of each in some detail; I hope that the questions raised here will prompt many readers to search for further enlightenment among the more specialized works available. Indeed, the growing number of sociological publications is strong evidence, I feel, for the increasingly constructive interest which many people, whether laymen or experts, are taking in the future shape of their own society.

The plan of this book was prepared with the idea that it would act as a basic source of material for the "Elements of Social Structure" optional paper in the University of London B.Sc. (Economics) degree, together with the "Social Structure of Modern Britain" paper in Part II of the same course and the B.A. and B.Sc. (Sociology) degrees. In addition, it will be found useful by those studying for the academic post-graduate Diploma in Public Administration (also a London University qualification), and by students of any branch of sociology, whether motivated by examination requirements or simply the layman's desire to acquire an understanding of the subject's main principles.

I am deeply indebted to Dr. A. H. Richmond, Professor of Sociology, York University, Toronto, for his constructive advice and criticism in the preparation of this book.

January 1964 E. A. J.

CHAPTER 1

Aspects of Population

And God spake unto Noah, saying, Go forth of the ark, thou, and thy wife, and thy sons, and thy sons' wives with thee. Bring forth with thee every living thing that is with thee, of all flesh, both of fowl, and of cattle, and of every creeping thing that creepeth upon the earth; that they may breed abundantly in the earth, and be fruitful, and multiply upon the earth.

(GENESIS viii. 16–17.)

POPULATION TRENDS IN THE TWENTIETH CENTURY

Apart from one unavoidable interruption in 1941, an unbroken series of decennial censuses stretches as far back as 1801. Although the first four are not strictly comparable because they do not include those members of the army, the navy, and the merchant service who were at home on the date of the census, the results can validly be compared for all normal purposes. Table 1* indicates the general growth of population in England and Wales since 1801, a period characterized by an enormous expansion in numbers, particularly in the early years of the last century. The reasons quoted for this are many and varied. Much emphasis has been placed, for example, on the culmination of that era in which agriculture was the basis of the social structure. It has been argued that the urban industrial worker found it easier, when the limitations of a peasant economy were removed, to set up a household of his own at an early age. Furthermore, the economic value of children in the first half of the nineteenth century must have encouraged large families to some degree. The most potent factor, however, was clearly the significant fall in infant

* Census of England and Wales, 1951, *General Tables*.

TABLE 1

Year	Population (thousands)	Average percentage increase over previous figure
1801	8,893	—
1851	17,928	20·3
1881	25,974	14·9
1891	29,003	11·7
1901	32,528	12·2
1911	36,070	10·9
1921	37,887	5·0
1931	39,952	5·5
1951	43,758	4·7

mortality for, according to an estimate for London published in the *Lancet* in 1835, the death rate for children was halved between 1750 and 1830. In the period up to 1750, nearly three-quarters of all children died before reaching 5 years of age; 100 years later the proportion dying was under one-third. Why did this falling mortality rate occur? Various explanations have been offered, including the spread of a purer water supply (although cholera epidemics broke out periodically throughout the century), vaccination, the general advance of medical knowledge and midwifery. As regards public health facilities, it is likely that after 1815 there was an actual worsening of conditions in the rapidly developing factory towns, for reasons which L. C. A. Knowles* sums up as follows:

> As there were no building restrictions houses were run up in any fashion, often back to back. There were no regulations to prevent overcrowding or cellar dwellings. There were no arrangements for disposing of the house refuse which always accumulates, ash-pits overflowed and spread a "layer of abomination" about the courts and streets; there was no system of main drainage and no system of sanitation. An adequate or clean water-supply laid on to the houses was rare until after 1850. The well and pumps were quite insufficient for the numbers who wished to use them and the river and canal water was polluted and disgusting.

Initially, too, the birth rate and infant survival were adversely affected by the fact that many expectant mothers had to work until the

* Knowles, L. C. A., *The Industrial and Commercial Revolutions.*

day of the birth of their children. In the mines, for instance, women often suffered distortions of the spine and pelvis which caused great difficulty at childbirth.*

Until the outbreak of World War I, the average size of the family had been fairly high, although the trend was obviously towards a reduction in the number of children. For those married in the period 1861 to 1869, the mean ultimate family size was 6·16; for couples married between 1900 and 1909, the equivalent figure was 3·3 children.† But the war had a far-reaching effect on family size, not only from the point of view of those husbands and fathers (both potential and actual) who were killed, but also because the ones who returned tended to have either very few children or none at all. Up to 1914, the average annual increase of the population, calculated in 10 year periods from official figures, had fluctuated around 1 per cent. After 1918, however, the figure fell to less than half, and did not rise again until after World War II. Since fewer babies were being born, it followed that older people would constitute a higher proportion of the total. In due course, it was argued, the population would actually decline, both absolutely and relatively, compared with the world at large. This view exemplifies the dangers of extrapolation from existing figures, for in fact statistics drawn from marriages taking place between 1935 and 1948 show a definite trend towards a larger family. The authors of the 1946 Family Census Report for the Royal Commission on Population‡ thought it very likely that "the marriages of 1941–7 will show some increase in fertility when their family sizes at ten years' duration can be measured".

* According to one woman quoted in the Report on Mines of 1842, a vast number of women "have dead children and false births, which are worse, as they are not able to work after the latter. I have always been obliged to work below till forced to go to bear the bairn, and so have all the other women. We return as soon as able, never longer than ten or twelve days; many less, if they are much needed."

† Figures from the Registrar-General, *Statistical Review*, 1957, Part III, Commentary. The original data were obtained at the 1911 Census and the 1946 Sample Family Census of the Royal Commission on Population.

‡ Glass, D. V., and Grebenik, E., *The Trend and Pattern of Fertility in Great Britain*, a Report on the Family Census of 1946, *Papers of the Royal Commission on Population*, vol. 6, 1954.

In the nineteenth century the population of Great Britain had swelled from about 10 million to about 37 million, and by 1939 it had increased to more than 46 million. Thus the basic theme, that of a growing populace, had been maintained almost continually since the beginning of the Industrial Revolution. The increase had provided a naturally expanding market both for the products of British industry and for imports of foodstuffs and raw materials from foreign countries. Towards the end of World War II it seemed that, at long last, the population was going to decline or remain static for a few years. G. D. H. Cole and Raymond Postgate,* for example, wrote:

> The population of England and Wales in 1939 was about 41,500,000. This figure was likely to increase for some short while, for the offspring of more prolific generations was in 1946 still with us. But the smaller generation, the generation of little families, was growing up to take their place. . . . It was almost certain that by 1951 the population would be something like two millions less than it was twenty years before.

These two authors draw some rather depressing economic conclusions from this estimate. Yet in fact, the 1951 census showed that the population of England and Wales was nearly 44½ million and, as if to emphasize the dangers of extrapolation even more strongly, the figures indicated a continuing rise. Whereas a couple marrying in 1940 would expect to have 2·00 children (an estimate based on the fertility rates for 1951–5), a couple marrying in 1952 might attain a mean ultimate family size of 2·18 children, which indicates a slight reversal of the tendency towards ever-smaller families. Moreover, if it is possible to make any forecasts on the basis of very recent figures, the Registrar-General's *Statistical Review*† for 1961 indicated that the 811,281 live births in that year were the highest since 881,026 in the "bulge" year of 1947, when many ex-servicemen were reunited with their wives after a long absence.‡ The birth rate in 1961,

* Cole, G. D. H., and Postgate, R., *The Common People, 1746–1946*, Methuen, London, second edition (revised), 1946.

† Registrar-General, *Statistical Review*, England and Wales, 1961, Part II, *Population Tables*.

‡ It has also been argued that the high birth rate immediately after 1945 was partly provoked by the intense demand for local authority housing. Couples with a large family stood a much greater chance of being allocated a council house, and some may have deliberately had children for this reason.

for each 1000 of the population, was 17·5, the highest since the 17·8 attained in 1948. This upward movement in births is regarded as so significant by the Government that all estimates of future needs are being radically revised. Originally, for example, it was forecast that the total number of children at school in 1985 would be nearly 2½ million more than those at school today; but this is almost certainly an excessively conservative calculation. The latest information from the Government Actuary suggests that the annual birth rate in the later 1960's will be between 50,000 and 60,000 higher than had been assumed. For similar reasons, the building programme for maternity hospitals has had to be amended. So hazardous has the business of population forecasting become, that in December 1963 the Government announced a detailed 10 per cent sample census for 1966 on the grounds that 10-year intervals are now too long for accurate planning.

The population of England and Wales in the middle of 1962 stood at 46,768,000. Apparently the large number of inaccurate forecasts of future population statistics in the past does not deter the Registrar-General from continuing to make these predictions, for the most recent extrapolations* allow for a total population in 2002 of 63,774,000, of which 32,194,000 would be males and 31,580,000 females. About one-third of the increase is attributed to a rise in the number of marriages and to marriage, particularly for women, at a younger age. The 221,952 births recorded in the first quarter of 1963 represented a rate of 19·3 per 1000 of the population; both the number and the rate were the highest for a first quarter since the peak year of 1947. This suggests that the Government's revised forecasts may be substantiated by a long-term tendency for larger families to be fashionable. It certainly seems logical to assume that, if improved standards of living continue to be accepted features of our society, then couples will not be deterred by economic factors from having several children. In addition, earlier marriages increase the potential period for pregnancies, although recent trends suggest that early marriage does not carry

* Registrar-General, *Quarterly Return*, No. 456, January–March 1963, H.M.S.O.

with it the likelihood of a large family to the same extent as formerly.*

Some remarkable things have been happening to the distribution of population, too.† The nineteenth century created an industrial system based on coal and iron, with the main population centres located in the northern counties, south Wales, and the Scottish industrial belt. In modern times, however, coal and iron play a much smaller part in determining the location of industry: electricity or gas have replaced coal as a direct source of power. Industries now tend to regard ports and markets as more potent factors in determining their choice of site. As a result, between 1921 and 1934 the population of London and the south-east rose by nearly 14 per cent, whereas the numbers in south Wales fell by 5 per cent. If a line could be drawn from Chester to Hull, it would be seen that approximately half of Britain lies to the north of that line and half to the south: the former half holds some 19 million and the latter about 32 million. The south—already far more densely populated—gained no less than five times as much population in the period 1951–61 as did the north. Specifically, the south-east is grabbing the lion's share of this increase and Hertfordshire, for instance, grew at a rate of 3·65 per cent *each year* over the same 10-year period. Some attempts have already been made to deal with the problem: the Distribution of Industry Acts and the 1960 Local Employment Act are intended to persuade any expanding industry to move northwards. Industrial Development Certificates—which give firms permission to expand on their existing sites—are at present being refused to companies in the south-east. The Government's development plans for the north-east and for central Scotland are deliberately designed to reverse present population movements.

Whereas in 1851 the population of England and Wales was evenly

* See Carr-Saunders, A. M., Jones, D. C., and Moser, C. A., *A Survey of Social Conditions in England and Wales*, Oxford University Press, 1958. In the 1900–9 cohort the average family size for women married between the ages of 40 and 44 was 51 per cent of that for women married between 20 and 24; for the 1925 cohort it was 72 per cent.

† For a more detailed analysis, see Carr-Saunders, A. M., Jones, D. C., and Moser, C. A., *op. cit.*, Chapter 5.

divided between urban and rural areas, the proportion had changed so much by 1901 that 75 per cent lived in towns, and in 1955 this had increased to more than four-fifths. Greater London alone accounts for 20 per cent of all the inhabitants of England and Wales. And the continuing expansion of all the urban areas is being accompanied by the steady depopulation of the country districts. In 1951 about 32 million acres of England and Wales were classed as rural, with an average of 0·25 persons per acre, and slightly over 5¼ million urban acres had a population density of 6·06 persons per acre. Naturally enough, the towns have spread farther and farther beyond their old municipal boundaries, as improved housing standards lead to increasing decentralization and the creation of suburbs. In the inter-war period, houses were built fewer to the acre, with more garden area, more parks and open spaces. This inevitably meant that most workers lived a considerable distance from their place of employment, so that travel expenses played a more important role in the family budget. Indeed, the development of suburban areas could not have occurred prior to the construction of railways and the emergence of cheap transport.

SOCIO-ECONOMIC ASPECTS OF POPULATION

An important aspect of population in this context is the way in which population changes can affect public finance. For analytical purposes the population can be subdivided into three distinct categories:

(1) Those below working age—calculated as all individuals below the age at which it is permissible to leave school.
(2) Those of working age—the age group 15–65 for men, and 15–60 for women.
(3) Those above working age—65 for men and 60 for women, although there are obvious exceptions to this rule.

The numbers in the first group have clearly increased substantially. Not only has there been an increase in the birth-rate, but the minimum school-leaving age has periodically been raised and opportunities for further education have been made available to a larger proportion of 15-year-olds. Nevertheless, in relative terms this category has tended to decrease in size and the third group has risen in numerical importance, for whereas 85 per cent of the dependent section of the population was under 15 in 1891, this proportion had declined to 62 per cent in 1955. If the Government assumes responsibility for those people who do not actively produce anything (i.e. children and old-age pensioners), then problems are going to occur if the numbers in these two groups increase in relation to those actually at work. Of recent years, the rate of expansion of the population within the working age group has been about 1 per cent compound, compared with an increase for the non-working population of 2·5 per cent compound. In percentage terms, the 1955 figures* indicate that the working population constituted 63·1 per cent of the total, children (22·6 per cent) and old dependents (14·3 per cent) together making up the remaining 36·9 per cent. Clearly a smaller number of productively employed citizens are being called upon to support a larger number of dependents. This must inevitably attract the attention of the Government responsible for supplying retirement pensions, child allowances, education, and other social services.

Fertility

One of the most conspicuous features of recent developments in the family is the growth and acceptance of the idea and practice of voluntary family limitations. Parents may deliberately control the number of births in their family with reference to the conditions and opportunities they can provide for their offspring, and the kind of life they themselves wish to lead. The undeniable decline in family size, since that era when the Victorians and their immediate predecessors reared families of an average size larger than those of any other period in British history, can be broadly illustrated by the fact that in 1881 the average family had between five and six children, whereas now it has (statistically) just over two. Growing preference for the smaller family is clearly indicated in Table 2.†

* Registrar-General, *Statistical Review of England and Wales*, H.M.S.O., 1955.

† Royal Commission on Population, *Papers*, VI, Table 2, H.M.S.O., 1949.

TABLE 2

Number of live births	Proportion of women (per 1000) with specified number of births, who were first married in		
	1870–9	1900–9	1925
0	83	113	161
1 or 2	125	335	506
3 or 4	181	277	221
5 to 9	434	246	106
10 or more	177	29	6
All	1000	1000	1000

One of the possible causes of this trend probably lies in the very sharp fall in infant mortality which occurred throughout the nineteenth century. The birth rate was indeed very high, and was rising up to the end of the 1860's, but what made the average family so unprecedently large at that time was the sudden propensity for survival among these numerous offspring. Hitherto, it had not been unusual for parents to lose in infancy or early childhood at least half its total number of, say, ten to twelve children. This appalling situation was alleviated by improvements in the standards of housing, sanitation, feeding, and medical knowledge generally. The decline in infant mortality first affected the middle classes,* since typically they enjoyed a higher standard of living and were better placed to take advantage of any improvements in social conditions. So it was not surprising that, having recovered from the initial shock of having eight children still alive out of ten, they were the first to take some positive action towards birth control.

The idea of family limitation was gaining ground in the last quarter of the nineteenth century. Although most of the propaganda on the subject was directed towards the masses, it somewhat naturally took effect first among those who could easily read and understand it. Ironically, then, it was the wealthy upper and upper-middle classes

* The terms "middle class" and "working class" are analysed more fully in Chapter 3.

which had the least economic incentive to control their families, which first began to do so. Thence the habit spread downwards to the middle classes proper, and finally to the skilled manual and lesser clerical workers. The twentieth century has completed the conversion of the middle classes to a small family pattern. As the Royal Commission on Population points out,* it is still true that the higher occupational groups practise birth control more diligently than the lower categories. Among couples married between 1900 and 1930, the families of manual workers were consistently about 40 per cent larger than those of non-manual workers; more recently, the average number of children in each category have been 2·5 and 1·7 respectively. Table 3† illustrates the comparative fecundity of the working classes in more detail, and shows that by 1931 the birth rate

TABLE 3

Class	Births per 1000 for families with husbands aged under 55 and wives under 45		
	1911	1921	1931
Professional and higher business	119	98	94
Lower professional and business ranks	132	104	90
Skilled workers	153	141	120
Semi-skilled workers	158	162	133
Unskilled workers	213	178	153

for the topmost class had been virtually stabilized, whereas for the lower groups it was still declining at a significant rate. Even now, as Willmott and Young‡ found in Bethnal Green, the old distrust of family limitation still lingers in some areas: a social worker persuaded a woman to have a contraceptive cap fitted, but two months later she was again pregnant, saying: "My husband wouldn't have it. He threw it on the fire."

* Royal Commission on Population, *Report* (Cmd. 7695), H.M.S.O., 1949.

† Quoted in Hubback, E. M., *The Population of Britain*, 1947.

‡ Young, M., and Willmott, P., *Family and Kinship in East London*, Routledge & Kegan Paul, London, 1957.

Although the use of contraceptives is not in itself a *cause* of birth control, but simply a *means* whereby the desired degree of family limitation may be obtained, it is true that the increased availability of chemical and mechanical methods of contraception have further contributed to the ideology of the small family. Contraceptives are available at most chemists and hairdressing shops for those not too embarrassed to ask for them, and there is no shortage of advice on how to use these implements. Some 284,000 people attended Family Planning Association clinics in Britain in 1961—there are nearly 400 of these establishments, all voluntarily staffed, most subsidized by the National Health Service and located on local authority or hospital premises. It is interesting to note that the F.P.A. is not solely concerned with encouraging family limitation: it also conducts research into infertility, on the grounds that 10 per cent of all marriages in Britain are involuntarily childless, a disappointing and frustrating situation which can lead to divorce.

Increased knowledge and discussion of birth control in the late nineteenth century were encouraged by the famous trial in 1877 of Bradlaugh and Mrs. Besant. Table 4 portrays subsequent developments in the use of all techniques for family limitation. Here again,

TABLE 4

Year of marriage	Percentage of wives with husbands in the following occupational groups who had used birth-control techniques			
	All non-manual workers	Skilled manual workers	Other manual workers	All classes
Before 1910	26	18	4	15
1910–19	60	39	33	40
1920–9	57	60	58	60
1930–9	68	65	67	64
1940–7	67	53	47	55

the comparative reticence of manual workers' families in this respect can be noted.

What were the motives in favour of restricting the number of children among middle-class families? The Royal Commission on Population lists a variety of reasons to account for this change in fashion, including, for example, the progressive emancipation of women and their attainment of equality with men in many fields. Certainly financial considerations could not have been paramount, for although the middle classes suffered a slight reversal of their economic fortunes in the 1870's—when the rate of increasing prosperity merely slowed down a little—their affluence in absolute terms was never seriously threatened. On the other hand, from being an economic asset in the early years of the nineteenth century, children rapidly became a financial liability. Rural prosperity decayed (and it became more difficult to rear a large brood), factory legislation limited and finally prevented the exploitation of child labour in industry, and education became compulsory. These changes probably affected the higher income groups some time before the last quarter of the century. As Banks* argues, although no single factor in the upbringing of children became markedly more expensive in this period, the cumulative effect of the increased cost of all the factors together was quite considerable. Even before education became compulsory, the gradual introduction of competitive examinations had made it more important for entrance into "gentlemanly" jobs. This in itself would not have been a major element in making children an economic liability, but it became so when the purely social differential was harder to maintain. At that stage, outlay for the children's future could no longer be skimped. The decision to restrict the size of one's family in order to provide all the children with "a good start in life" is to be distinguished as a motive from the restriction of families in order to maintain the material standard of living of the parents.

This latter consideration must be of vital importance in view of the fact that, other things being equal, the competitive struggle for goods and services is a race in which the advantage lies with the childless couple. Added to this are the extraneous influences of increased leisure opportunities coupled with the large number of

* Banks, J. A., *Prosperity and Parenthood*, Routledge & Kegan Paul, London, 1954.

leisure pursuits being commercially exploited (of which the car may perhaps be described as the most pervasive). Since these all cost money, the economic incentive to limit families is further intensified. As the leisure activities, clothing fashions, and general style of life of the upper classes permeate through to the masses, aided by the large-scale media of communication, so these upper-class characteristics become more visible and more desirable. The conscious desire to achieve upward social mobility is a relatively recent phenomenon, but it is a pre-requisite of achieving this aim that the individual should adopt the morals of the social class he wishes to enter. Because the neo-Malthusian birth-control propagandists directed their warnings on the dangers of excessive fecundity mainly to the poor, it is scarcely remarkable that increasing numbers of "status-dissenting" lower-class people began to regard the practice of "breeding like rabbits" as a despicable habit, to be eschewed by the *élite*.

Again, the considerably improved status of women did more than weaken the traditional supremacy of the male. It also concentrated anxious attention on the welfare of expectant mothers and young children. The old attitude of: "If the women complained, it was hold your noise and give her another baby"* has been generally replaced by an arrangement where, in Ronald Fletcher's words,† "Women now enter marriage on a completely voluntary basis and on an equal footing with their male partners. This improved status has meant, of course, that many women no longer wish to be confined to a life of child-bearing, child-rearing, and domesticity." The feminist movement was directed largely against the subordinate status of women in the middle classes but, as in so many other social changes, its effects were eventually felt in all sections of the community. Furthermore, the emancipation of women has its economic implications inasmuch as if wives demand to pursue their own independent aims and interests, these may cost money and the family may feel compelled to sacrifice the desire for more children.

* An informant quoted in Young, M., and Willmott, P., *op. cit.*
† Fletcher, R., *The Family and Marriage*, Penguin Books, 1962.

In 1949 Lewis-Faning* reported to the Royal Commission on Population that early marriage was one of the most important factors tending to produce a large family, and this view was accepted by the Commission. Certainly there may have been some truth in this assertion during the nineteenth century, when the rapid development of industrialization forced a decline in the number of apprenticeships offered and a compensating increase in the proportion of urban workers who began to earn a full wage when scarcely out of adolescence. The 1840 Report of the Poor Law Commissioners remarks that many 18-year-old youths "assumed the most important office of manhood" and consequently had adequate time to acquire a vast collection of children. On the other hand, it seems more likely that in recent years couples have been concentrating their births into the early years of marriage, a possibility which would give the short-term illusion that the birth rate was rising. The extent of the illusion would only become apparent with the availability of the figures for family size after, say, 15 years of marriage. If the birth rate were actually rising significantly, one would expect the increase to be correlated with marriage duration: the longer the marriage, the larger the family. In fact, the correlation is not very marked.†

The view that a decline in reproductive capacity may have accounted for the declining birth rate has definitely been dismissed. It seems to have been finally discredited by the slight upward trend in fertility during the past few years. For this a number of reasons may be responsible. Just as the end of the nineteenth century saw a reaction against the over-large family, perhaps the current trend represents a reaction against the over-small one. It appears that the change is once again being led by the middle classes, for the working class is still in the economizing stage and this prevailing morality does not encourage the acquisition of offspring (although the 1951 census showed that Class 5 families, in the Registrar-General's fivefold classification, averaged 3·18 children compared with 1·88

* Lewis-Faning, E., *Family Limitation and its Influence on Human Fertility during the past Fifty Years*, Papers of the Royal Commission on Population, H.M.S.O., 1949.

† See footnote on p. 6.

for Class 1 households). While there may be some evidence for the decrease in the marginal utility of expenditure in the direction of material possessions, it is more speculative to hypothesize in terms of the uncertainties of the modern world, which may lead couples to seek security in family life. It seems equally likely that a decline in the birth rate could be attributed to the same cause. On the other hand, recent thinking on family relationships has suggested that the development of individual personality and character may benefit from membership within a larger family. From the economic viewpoint, too, the costs of childbearing have declined, from £15 in 1930 (for doctor's fees alone) to nil. In addition, helpful grants are available, such as the £22 maternity allowance for all mothers.

Figures given in the previous paragraph from the 1951 census give some data on differential fertility between social classes. The signs are that this is becoming less marked: the size of non-manual workers' families has remained the same, whereas the number of children typically sired by working-class families has continued to decline. This suggests that the former have reached stability while the latter have not. But if the fact is accepted that there is a substantial difference between the average fertility of the various social classes, then the social consequences of these differences must be considered.

Before World War II, because of the widespread belief that the population was being recruited largely from those parents with below-average intelligence, it was predicted that the ability of the country as a whole, as measured by I.Q., would decline by about two points per generation. After that war, however, similar studies (chiefly on Scottish schoolchildren) in fact revealed a slight gain in average test intelligence. This does not necessarily mean that the original hypothesis was wrong for, as Professor Cyril Burt wrote in 1950, the reliability of intelligence tests (as indicators of innate intelligence) might be questioned. Also, the children might be more familiar with such tests, and such sophistication would produce falsely high scores. Undoubtedly, intelligence test results are only a partial guide to ability, and since intelligence itself is not a unitary factor, it cannot be easily isolated. Moreover, a drastic re-appraisal of the nature of intelligence itself has largely demolished the pessimistic arguments on the relationship between "innate" ability and differential fertility. In the words of *The Newsom Report*:*

> Intellectual talent is not a fixed quantity with which we have to work but a variable that can be modified by social policy and educational approaches . . . the kind of intelligence which is measured by the tests so far applied is largely an acquired characteristic. This is not to deny the existence of a basic genetic endowment; but whereas that endowment, so far, has proved impossible to isolate, other factors can be identified. Particularly significant among them are the influences of social and physical environment; and, since these are susceptible to modification, they may well prove educationally more important.

Opinions may legitimately differ on whether culture (which is, in any case, an intangible and non-measurable quality) exists in a greater degree among the upper and middle classes; T. S. Eliot† would agree with this proposition, while Richard Hoggart‡ would not. But even supposing that the upper and middle classes are not reproducing themselves, this does not automatically mean that their cultural values will disappear. One of the most widely remarked phenomena of this period is the more overtly expressed preference of the working classes for a middle-class style of life. Furthermore, the problem may be solving itself: the practice of family limitation is gaining ground consistently in the working class, and that section of society which is held to possess a higher average level of "intelligence" and culture is in the process of abandoning its drastic adoption of strict birth-control procedures.§ The combination of these two effects may eventually cancel out the allegedly adverse effects of differential fertility.

* The Newsom Report, *Half our Future*, a report of the Central Advisory Council for Education (England), H.M.S.O., 1963.

† See, for example, Eliot, T. S., *Notes Towards a Definition of Culture*, Faber & Faber, London.

‡ Hoggart, R., *The Uses of Literacy*, Chatto & Windus, London, 1957.

§ See Hubback, E. M., *op. cit.*: "One hopeful sign is that among a small section of the professional classes there is a definite tendency to have a family—and still more to want to have a family—of four children. Future trends will obviously be affected if this tendency is maintained and spreads to other and larger sections of the population."

Mortality

According to the P.E.P. report, *World Population and Resources,** death control should proceed hand-in-hand with birth control. But, because the former generally precedes the latter, and because death control is generally regarded as beneficial, while birth control is subject to hostility from large sections of the populace, world population has been accelerating rapidly. In this country, mortality for all age groups is declining steadily, although there must eventually come a time when the death rate is stabilized. The drugs introduced in this century (particularly the anti-biotics like penicillin) have increased the over-all expectation of life, but eventually senescence—the run-down of the brain and heart—takes its toll. The 526,268 deaths occurring in 1960 gave a crude death rate of 11·5 per thousand of the population.† In the 10 years from 1950 to 1960, there had been an 11 per cent decline in mortality, when account is taken of age changes in the distribution of the population (with a larger number of people reaching old age, crude death rates may even rise slightly, giving a misleading impression of actual trends).

The decline in deaths during infancy and early childhood is still declining and at present is the lowest ever recorded. Infant deaths are concentrated in the last stages of pregnancy, at birth, and during the next few days. It is interesting to note that more infants are lost by being still-born and by dying in the first year of life than children and adults during the next 40 years. These early mortalities are primarily caused by congenital defects, injury at birth, etc., while deaths after the first week are caused by respiratory infections, accidents, alimentary infections, all of which are correlated strongly with adverse social factors and environment. Hence the further reduction of the infant death rate presents social as well as medical problems. Indeed, although the number of infant deaths has declined for all social groups, the differential between the upper and lower classes has not been removed, so that there are still substantial variations in life-chances for babies born in families at each level in the

* *World Population and Resources,* Political and Economic Planning, London, 1955.

† Registrar-General, *Statistical Review 1960,* H.M.S.O., 1961.

social scale. The authors of *Growing Up in Newcastle Upon Tyne** admit that many parents still live in unsatisfactory or overcrowded houses and suffer from personal instability or frustration. It is precisely these factors which are coming into greater prominence now that the more serious illnesses are coming under control, that primary poverty has almost disappeared, and that standards of hygiene, nutrition and education are arising.† It is argued that "the health of children and the outcome of disease are closely related to family environment." A "good" environment is specifically defined as including "a sound dwelling of sufficient size,‡ a reasonable income wisely used, and parents who enjoy a satisfying relationship with each other and are sensitive to their children's needs". All these attributes, it will be noted, are at present most easily acquired by middle-class families. If nothing else, they generally have an income sufficient to obtain a satisfactory residence, and an income, moreover, which tends to remain stable from month to month. This gives the salaried employee an inestimable advantage over his wage-paid counterpart in planning his long-term spending.

Infectious diseases in infancy and childhood are inevitable among children of all social classes, but the risk of death has been considerably reduced; even such characteristically fatal illnesses as diphtheria, tuberculosis and polio are now virtually under control. On the other hand, the falling death rate from these causes has only emphasized the number of permanent disabilities and handicaps left by the illnesses of infancy and early childhood. These include mental deficiency, deafness, defects of vision, etc. in which con-

* Miller, Court, Walton and Knox, *Growing Up in Newcastle Upon Tyne.*

† Certainly the practices reported in the 1843 Report of the Children's Employment Commission have now entirely disappeared—in that document, the Nottingham coroner was quoted as saying that "Godfrey's Cordial", a preparation of opium given to infants to keep them quiet, was often administered on the day of birth, with the result that "a great number of infants perish. . . . Those who escape with life become pale and sickly children, often half idiotic, and always with a ruined constitution".

‡ See Carr-Saunders, A. M., Jones, D. C., and Moser, C. A., *op. cit.* The 1951 figures analysed in this book show that 6 per cent of all households in England and Wales were without piped water in that year; the same percentage was without a kitchen sink; as many as 37 per cent were without a fixed bath.

genital factors play a much smaller part than was formerly thought. Where infectious diseases do occur, resulting in death or in deformities which may go unnoticed for many years, their incidence is higher in homes where the income is either inadequate or irregular or both, where the parents are ignorant of their responsibilities, and where the very multiplicity of children makes it impossible for any single sufferer to be granted enough attention. Such homes belong almost invariably to members of the lower social classes, although their numbers are declining with the spread of full employment, increasing standards of education and literacy, the dissemination of child-care knowledge through the media of child welfare clinics, periodicals, broadcasting, etc., to say nothing of advances in medical facilities and techniques. The State provides family allowances to help maintain the child; prenatal and postnatal care is available for mother and child. Far from diminishing the family's responsibilities in this direction, these State agencies have supplemented the family's prime concern for the health of its members, so that families, if anything, are faced with more exacting demands.

At the other end of the spectrum, the figures show that, despite significant increases in the death rate from such diseases as coronary thrombosis and cancer (especially lung cancer), the proportion of old people in the population is steadily rising. This has been a continuing process in Britain for more than 70 years: between 1891 and 1947, the percentage of old people over 60 years had doubled itself, from 7 to 15 per cent. Unless unpredictable factors intervene, this ageing of the population will continue and become more apparent before the end of the present century. The most recent estimates of the Registrar-General* suggest that whereas the present proportion of old-age pensioners (men 65 and over, women 60 and over) is 14·9 per cent of the total, this figure will have risen by 1982 to 16·4 per cent. Then it should decline to 15·6 per cent in 1992 and to 14·3 per cent in 2002—but in the bigger population of 2002 (there is an estimated figure of 63,774,000), pensioners would number 9,107,000, as against 6,985,000 in 1963.

* Registrar-General, *Quarterly Return No. 456*, January–March 1963, H.M.S.O.

From the viewpoint of public finance, these trends imply that if the population contains an increasing percentage of old people, they may become an economic burden on those who are productively employed. Perhaps a consoling feature of this argument is that the current rate of increase in the Gross National Product is thought to be sufficient to support that section of the population which is consuming but not producing, and still leave enough for an increase in general standards of living.

Old age is a biological term rather than a social category. The influence of the various old-age pension measures has tended to create a widespread impression that everyone aged 65 or over is automatically "old" in every sense of the word, and that retirement is simply a period during which the individual can decay in peace. Most superannuation schemes are based on job retirement at certain ages, regardless of the degree of senescence reached. Some schemes do provide for an extension of the working period to the age of, say, 75, but this kind of provision invariably meets with criticism from younger men whose promotion is accordingly postponed. On the other hand, if considerations of higher productivity should prompt the Government to raise the qualifying age for pensions, such a move would arouse heated opposition from people who do not particularly like their work and look forward to retirement. Manual work, for example, might come into this category, and for manual workers to continue in employment after a certain age, some re-training would be necessary. However, this is not an insuperable obstacle. The idea that older people are incapable of learning anything new is steadily being discredited; although they may take longer to acquire new techniques, they can do so in time. People are usually trained for their work in their teens and early twenties, and one of the prevailing myths of job-training is that learning is more difficult for those of middle age; fortunately, the available facts do not give unqualified support to this assumption.*

* Since 1952, the Rubery Owen organization, of Darlaston, Staffs., has established a separate workshop for older employees aged 70 or more. Operating on a commercial basis, the scheme has achieved considerable success, but it is, of course, an honourable exception to the general rule. The company has found these older workers to be extraordinarily amenable

Despite the fact that older people may be slower, this does not necessarily mean that they are inefficient; older workers tend to establish a steady routine, so that, in the long run, their output may be higher than that of younger men. World War II, when the percentage of employed persons aged over 65 more than doubled itself, revealed conclusively that the so-called disabilities of old age are largely imaginary. Rowntree's study of the subject, published by the Nuffield Foundation in 1947, stated that only in very few cases was it found necessary to raise piece-rates or pay old workers lower hourly rates on grounds of their low output. If any adjustment on account of age was necessary, it usually took the form of lighter work rather than of reduced working hours. A third of the firms participating in the study said that absenteeism was lower among the old workers. It was generally agreed that while these employees could hold their own as regards conscientiousness and efficiency, they were handicapped by their slower speed. The Rowntree Committee concluded that if retirement were postponed, this might be beneficial to the individual because it would delay the effects of ageing, and beneficial to the nation in that it would keep down the proportion of non-producers in the population. Furthermore, if workers were encouraged to remain in employment after the current retirement age, their degree of dependence on younger relatives would be significantly reduced. In an ageing population such as ours, job mobility is more rigid—it is less easy for the young to move into new industries and new localities, simply because the old (their dependants) lack mobility.

How well are old people cared for? A good deal of assistance is now provided by the State or by agencies working under the supervision of local authorities—old people's bungalows and flats, meals-on-wheels, and pensions themselves, which were not introduced into this country until 1908. This has similarly led to the charge that families no longer feel responsible for looking after their aged

---

to re-training, provided they are not taught by conventional classroom methods. It is interesting to note that in his 1963 Budget speech, the Chancellor of the Exchequer announced a £10 million allocation for the development of jobs re-training centres, mostly in north-east England.

members. As a consequence, the old people feel neglected and discarded, a feeling which is unmercifully accentuated by their forced retirement at 65 when in fact they still feel reasonably fit and active. There is some evidence for this view, but there is also evidence pointing to the contrary conclusion, since if the allegation of increasing neglect were wholly true, one would expect the proportion of old people in institutions for the aged to be rising sharply. In fact, according to Brian Abel-Smith and Robert Pinker,* "Despite much higher standards of social welfare, much smaller families, and above all a lengthening of life among the 'institutionally prone', society was not carrying a larger institutional 'burden' in 1951 than in 1911." It is unfortunate that many new housing developments undertaken by local government authorities do not include any (or enough) provision for older relatives, with the result that the isolation between different generations of the same family is artificially increased.† Clearly much more constructive thought and action is required before old age ceases to bear its stigma of decrepitude and negativism, and becomes instead a phase of life containing positive pleasures and greater security.

* Abel-Smith, B., and Pinker, R., *Changes in the Use of Institutions in England and Wales between 1911 and 1951*, Paper to the Manchester Statistical Society, 10 February 1960.

† See Young, M., and Willmott, P., *op. cit.*, for a detailed account of the effects of the transition from old-established neighbourhood (Bethnal Green) to virgin housing estate.

CHAPTER 2

The Family

Marriage is but keeping house, Sharing food and company.

(W. J. TURNER, *Epithalamium*)

What therefore God hath joined together, let no man put asunder . . . Whosoever shall put away his wife and marry another, committeth adultery against her.

INTRODUCTION

Just as the atom is the basic unit of physical structure so the family is the basic unit of our social structure. It is only necessary to glance at the immense amount of literature which has been published on the subject of the family in order to obtain an impression of the high esteem in which it is held in our value system. Today, in particular, a great deal of attention is being given to, and has arisen out of, an attempt to establish the existence of a family "problem": its loss of functions, the fall in the birth rate, the abandonment of the aged, the increasing rates of divorce, desertion, crime and illegitimacy, the rise in the number of children under the care of local authorities, the increasing number of mothers out at work. All these "facts", and more, have been cited in support of the argument that unless drastic action is taken, the family will collapse in ruins. Bertrand Russell,* on the one hand, can refer to "the decay of the family", and the Rev. E. C. Urwin† can state that "The family is declared to have failed both in its primary function of caring for

* Russell, B., *Marriage and Morals*, Allen & Unwin, London, 1932.
† Urwin, Rev. E. C., *The Way of a Christian Citizen*, Epworth, London, 1946.

children and as a source of human happiness". Dr. Ronald Fletcher,* by contrast, concludes that

> If we take . . . the "essential" functions of the family—the satisfaction of the sexual needs of the married couple, the careful upbringing of children, and the provision of a satisfactory home for its members—it is perfectly clear that the modern family—entailing the equal status of wife and husband and their mutual consideration in marriage; the high status of children; and the improved standards of income, housing, household equipment—aims at, and achieves, a far more satisfactory and refined provision for these needs than did either the pre-industrial family or the family of early industrial Britain, in which women were inferior and subjected, women and children were frequently exploited within or outside the family, and conditions in the home were so deplorably inadequate.

Part of the purpose of this chapter is to examine the validity of these clearly incompatible opinions, and to arrive at a more objective synthesis.

THE FAMILY TODAY

In non-industrial societies, as M. Penelope Hall† points out, the family's duties include provision of the necessities of life, care of the old, and education of the young. These duties are not only the concern of the family itself, but also of the whole kinship group. R. M. MacIver‡ writes that the pre-industrial family was a "multi-functional" unit, to a large extent self-governing, performing its own religious functions, responsible for its children's education, and providing an economic basis for the home, with all that this implies. He further argues that, with the development of complex industrialization, certain "non-essential" functions have been taken over by specialized agencies operating outside the sphere of the family. Government has been taken over by the State, religion by the Church, education by a publicly sponsored system of schools—and the growth of the factory system means that the family has ceased to be an economic unit. This being so, the family in an industrial society

* Fletcher, R., *The Family and Marriage*, Penguin Books, 1962.

† Hall, M. P., *The Social Services of Modern England*, Routledge & Kegan Paul, London, 1960.

‡ MacIver, R. M., and Page, C. N., *Society*, Macmillan, London, 1957.

is left with three "essential" functions, tasks which it alone can perform, namely, "Provision of a home. Production and rearing of children. Stable satisfaction of sex need." MacIver suggests that, since the family has been relieved of the burden of its "non-essential" duties, it may concentrate more completely on the satisfactory accomplishment of these three primary needs.

By contrast, the view currently held by many eminent writers is that the family has been stripped of the functions which are essential to its cohesion, and that parents have abnegated their responsibilities in favour of the government-run organs of the Welfare State. Rumney and Maier* write that

> The significance of the family as a social institution may be measured by the number of basic functions it performs . . . the functions of the modern family are few. All but gone are its economic, educational, religious, and protective functions. They have been transferred to the State, the Church, the school, and industry.

While arguments of this kind are difficult to quantify, convincing evidence could also be adduced to show that, in fact, standards of parental care have never been higher, since the services provided by the State have merely brought home to parents the importance of such matters as health and education.

Sprott† argues that "The family, under Western cultural conditions, has shrunk functionally" and that the social services are basically "anti-family" in that they cater almost exclusively for the *individual* rather than for the family as a whole. This view is supported up to a point by M. Penelope Hall‡ when she quotes the article on *Social Policy and the Family* from the Report§ of the Royal Commission on Population. This document remarks that the family has, until recently, been given only a minor place in social policy, "and the over-all effect has been to lower the status of the family in the national life". Day nurseries and school meals, for example, encourage a mother to go out to work, but do not encourage her to

* Rumney and Maier, *The Science of Society*.
† Sprott, W. J. H., *Sociology*, Methuen, London.
‡ Hall, M. P., *op. cit.*
§ Royal Commission on Population, *Report* (Cmd. 7695), 1949.

create a home for her children. While family ties may be undermined by this kind of welfare provision, M. Penelope Hall still concludes that the individual must be the State's chief concern, for part of the purpose of the social services is to protect the immature, the neglected and the ill-treated from their own families or relatives. However, even if the individual is the basis of the Welfare State, is it a fair accusation to level at the social services that they have been responsible, in Carl C. Zimmerman's phrase* for the family's "present rapid trend toward a climactic break-up"? In reality, the post-1945 social security measures have done much to relieve economic pressures on the family and so preserve its unity.

Another aspect of the declining functions of the family hypothesis concerns recreation which, says MacIver,† is no longer self-created and enjoyed in the home by the members of the family, but is increasingly provided outside the family by agencies such as clubs and the cinema. Unfortunately, the comfortable cliché of Victorian leisure as one long musical soirée is very remote from reality. Only a comparatively small percentage of households could afford a piano and, moreover, in working-class homes there were no such things as mutually shared pleasures among husbands and wives. As Willmott and Young‡ have pointed out, in their study of East London families, working-class housing was formerly so overcrowded, dirty and uncomfortable that husbands were glad to get away to the pub. It cost a good deal, measured in glasses of beer, to rent a seat at the pub, so very often the housekeeping allowance had to suffer. As one informant said, "From the home point of view there was no enjoyment at all for the man, so when he did get a bit of money he tended to go round to the pub and spend it there." Today, housing conditions have improved so much (in Bethnal Green, the number living more than 2 in a room has declined from 1 in 3 in 1911 to 3 in 100 in 1951) that husbands no longer need to escape to the pub, and they are more likely to "fetch a bottle in, so they can watch the telly

* Zimmerman, C. C., *Family and Civilization*, Harper, New York and London, 1947.

† MacIver, R. M., and Page, C. N., *op. cit.*

‡ Young, M., and Willmott, P., *Family and Kinship in East London*, Routledge & Kegan Paul, London, 1957.

at the same time". It is dangerous to make any definitive assertions about the use of leisure, but the increasing adoption of the 5-day working week* and the introduction of labour-saving devices in the home both mean that families have more leisure time. The characteristically democratic structure of most modern families means that husbands and wives spend more of this time together.

Yet another fashionable generalization concerning the family is that it has been reduced to its nuclear essentials in recent years. C. A. R. Crosland† argues that whereas, in Victorian times, the family was regarded as the entire sum of different generations (any photograph of an elaborately posed nineteenth-century group will support this remark), today one thinks of the family as simply the parents and their dependent children. Crosland goes on to attribute this change, at least in part, to the comparatively novel features in our society of occupational mobility and housing developments (suburbs, new housing estates and new towns). Talcott Parsons,‡ in the U.S.A., also cites high geographical and occupational mobility as the factors responsible. Support for the generalization itself comes from such studies as J. M. Mogey's *Family and Neighbourhood*,§ which explores the differences between Barton, a new housing estate near Oxford, and the older, neighbourhood-centred society of St. Ebbe's. Interviews showed that husband and wife in Barton shared more activities in the household daily routine—families would go for a joint holiday for the first time; more husbands and wives went

* *Family and Kinship in East London* proves this point: "The reduction of working hours after 1918, and again after 1945, has made a difference to every family. The spread of the five-day week has created the 'week-end', a new term and a new experience for the working man. With it has come the sight of young fathers wheeling prams up Bethnal Green Road on a Saturday morning, taking their little daughters for a row on the lake or playing with their sons on the putting green." Note, too, the powerful campaigns for a 40-hour week in the building and engineering industries in 1962–3, opposed by the Government on economic grounds but still indicative of an inevitable trend.

† Crosland, C. A. R., *The Future of Socialism*, Cape, London, 1956.

‡ Parsons, T., *Essays in Sociological Theory Pure and Applied*, Glencoe, Ill., Free Press, U.S.A., 1949.

§ Mogey, J. M., *Family and Neighbourhood*, Oxford University Press, 1956.

walking with their children. It appeared that the housing estate encouraged the nuclear family as distinct from the extended family. In the latter, the mother, married daughter and children form one clique, while the husband is expected to spend much of his time with other men in the locality. Homans,* too, writes that extended kinship has tended to disappear because it has fewer uses: the nuclear family moves more frequently and relatives are rarely available to fill their traditional functions, such as baby-sitting.

While this emphasis on the nuclear network may be true of some families, however, it is by no means true of all. Class differences probably account for some significant variations from the norm. So far as the working class is concerned, for instance, Willmott and Young† discovered that, in the East End of London, "the extended family is still very much a reality" and they speak of "a living extended family which includes within it three, and even four, generations". Ties were especially strong between mother, daughter and grandchildren, so much so that prospective husbands have to learn two roles: that of son-in-law as well as that of husband. The same authors' similar study of Woodford,‡ a middle-class London suburb, indicated that there was less emphasis on kinship than in Bethnal Green, and more emphasis on friendship. This trend has parallels in the U.S.A. ,and perhaps suggests that the contemporary movement towards the nuclear family is almost exclusively a middle-class phenomenon. Certainly the housing authorities, having moved many Bethnal Green families to housing estates without regard to kinship affiliations, had aroused much opposition in the area. Willmott and Young make a plea for the reconstruction of urban areas rather than the indiscriminate movement of families to dormitory estates. Many social workers in Bethnal Green were engaged in caring for mothers who had been left behind when their married daughters moved away from the area.

Further support for the extended family hypothesis derives from

* Homans, G. C., *The Human Group*, Harcourt Brace, New York, 1950.

† Young, M., and Willmott, P., *Family and Kinship in East London.*

‡ Young, M., and Willmott, P., *Family and Class in a London Suburb*, Routledge & Kegan Paul, London, 1960.

the slight positive tendency for women, when married, to set up home near their relatives, rather than near their husbands' relatives. Mays,* writing of the Liverpool dockland, says that "a mile can be thought of as a wide separation", and Clancy Sigal's *Weekend in Dinlock*† shows the importance of kinship ties in a mining area.

The last words on this question, however, come from Geoffrey Gorer,‡ who concludes:

> People in the working class outside the southern counties of England do tend to live near their kinsfolk; it is the people of the south, especially the middle class . . . who are most often separated from their kith and kin and therefore dependent on friends and neighbours for help and companionship.

Moreover, it would be hard to refute Dr. Ronald Fletcher's suggestion§ that

> in localities (urban and rural alike) in which a strong community life and spirit has continued—as in Bethnal Green, in the villages of the Forest of Dean, in small mining towns—the inter-relationships and the degree of mutual aid between the family and wider kindred may still continue to be of importance. In the larger conurbations, in suburbs, in growing dormitory areas, and in New Towns, however, the distance between the individual family and its wider kindred is likely to be much more marked.

"Production and rearing of children" is one of the essential functions of the family, according to MacIver. The socialization of the child has attracted considerable attention from social psychologists,‖ since it is during its formative years that the child acquires the foundations of its future way of life. Several American studies of child-rearing have pointed to class variations, but the material is somewhat complicated by ethnic and cultural differences. B. M. Spinley's study of socialization in a London slum, *The Deprived and*

* Mays, J. B., *Growing Up in the City*, Liverpool University Press, 1954.

† Sigal, C., *Weekend in Dinlock*, Secker & Warburg, London, 1960.

‡ Gorer, G., *Exploring English Character*, Cresset Press, 1955.

§ Fletcher, R., *op. cit.*

‖ Especially Gesell, A., *The First Five Years of Life*, Methuen, London, 1940; Valentine, C. W., *The Normal Child*, Penguin Books, 1956; Bridges, K. M. B., *The Social and Emotional Development of the Pre-School Child*, Routledge & Kegan Paul, London, 1931; Bossard, J. H., *The Sociology of Child Development*, Harper, New York, 1948.

*the Privileged,** reveals the inconsistent methods of training employed by working-class parents, admittedly in an atypical area. At an early age, the child is sent out to play in the street, and he quickly becomes a member of what Dr. Robb† calls "a unisexual gang of boys of his own age". It is important to note that the influence of the gang—with its own hierarchical structure and group norms—is directly competitive with that of the home. Working-class children do not regard their homes as places in which to spend their leisure time—according to Mays,‡ writing of the Liverpool dock area, "over the age of twelve, boys do not spend much time in the home, except when they are sick".

The lack of restraint which surrounds the working-class child means that he is less able to cope with stress situations—yet, ironically, as Terence Morris§ points out, he will encounter more of such situations, because he usually has to bring up a family on a limited, possibly irregular, income, and money disagreements may be one of the most potent sources of marital discord.

By contrast, the middle-class child is normally reared in a carefully controlled way: his feeds are regulated, his periods of rest and play are subject to a firm discipline. Play is restricted to the house or garden, and the street play group scarcely exists—indeed, J. M. Mogey's *Family and Neighbourhood*|| shows that one of the effects of the housing estate is that parents dislike their children playing in the street in case they pick up undesirable habits or accents.

With regard to the arrangements made for the care of children by mothers at work, several studies have shown that conditions have markedly improved since the 1843 Children's Employment Commission,¶ referring to domestic workers, stated that "married women, having no time to attend to their families, or even to suckle

* Spinley, B. M., *The Deprived and the Privileged,* Routledge & Kegan Paul, London, 1953.

† Robb, J. H., *Working-Class Anti-Semite,* Tavistock Publications, London, 1954.

‡ Mays, J. B., *op. cit.*

§ Morris, T., *The Criminal Area*, Routledge & Kegan Paul, London, 1957.

|| Mogey, J. M., *op. cit.*

¶ Quoted in Fletcher, R., *op. cit.*

their offspring, freely administer opium in some form or other to their infants, in order to prevent their cries interfering with the protracted labour by which they strive to obtain a miserable subsistence". Writing of the work done by females in the coal mines, Dr. Pinchbeck* remarks:

> The tragedy was that "the savage rudeness" of the upbringing of girls in the pits was not counteracted by any system of education. Introduced into the pit in early childhood before any correct ideas of conduct could be formed, they gradually grew accustomed to obscene language, vice, and debauchery.

Today, it is not only true that children are valued more (even though their economic value is nil), but also arrangements for their proper care are easier to make. Whereas in the nineteenth century, for instance, it was not exceptional for a mother who had just had a baby to return to work after about four weeks, in modern times the relieving of economic pressures has reduced to negligible proportions the number of women at work with children under 1 year old. Furthermore, mothers may choose between a wide variety of facilities available: day nurseries, nursery schools (operated by the local authority or by factories themselves), neighbours, childminders, mothers or mothers-in-law. Zweig† indicates that placing the child with Granny is more common, for reasons which recall our earlier mention of the importance of the extended family. One mother said that "Granny is like a mother to them and more experienced than I am". The general consensus of opinion was that Granny could give the child personal attention and love, while the nursery could only give professional expertise. Conditions favour the proper care of children in other respects, too: families are smaller in number, which means that each child can obtain more consideration and attention; greater longevity means a larger supply of Grannies. Finally, the eagerness with which factories seek women employees is reflected in their willingness to make special arrange-

* Pinchbeck, I., *Women Workers and the Industrial Revolution, 1750–1850*, Routledge & Kegan Paul, London, 1930.

† Zweig, F., *Women's Life and Labour*, Gollancz, London.

ments, either by setting up nurseries of their own, or by operating specially timed shifts to cater for mothers with young children.*

THE POSITION OF WOMEN

The achievement of political equality for women in the early twentieth century was accompanied by a considerable measure of effective social equality.† Women now have recognized rights with regard to the ownership of property; educational opportunity; entry to many occupations. They now enter marriage on a completely voluntary basis and on an equal footing with their male partners. While this has been a laudable development in many respects, it has brought new problems in its train. For example, whereas the husband in Victorian families automatically made the decisions and had complete control, today the refusal to accept this practice has caused some vagueness over what should be the individual responsibilities of husband and wife. Young and Willmott,‡ in their survey of Bethnal Green, found that 32 of the 45 husbands in the marriage sample gave some assistance with the housework; 29 had done the washing-up at least once in the week previous to the interview. They note that Booth and Rowntree, in their surveys of London and York respectively, made half a century earlier, do not mention washing-up, probably because in 1900 there was no question about it.

* For example, the biscuit factory in Bermondsey reported by Jephcott, P., Seear, N., and Smith, J., *Married Women Working*, Allen & Unwin, London, 1962.

† In the nineteenth century, as Professor R. H. Graveson points out: "On marriage all the wife's personal chattels became the absolute property of the husband, while the husband could dispose of the wife's leasehold property during his life and enjoyed for his own benefit her freehold estate during her life . . . the married woman, both physically and economically, was very much in the position of a chattel of her husband" (Graveson, R. H., and Crane, F. R. (Eds.), *A Century of Family Law*, 1857–1957, Sweet & Maxwell, London, 1957). These sentiments are echoed by O. R. McGregor (*Divorce in England*, Heinemann, London, 1957): "Outside the family, married women had the same legal status as children and lunatics; within it they were their husband's inferiors. By marriage they moved from dependence on fathers or male relatives to dependence on husbands."

‡ Young, M., and Willmott, P., *op. cit.*

On the wife's part, too, there is a growing demand for leisure, particularly at weekends; and although this may seem trivial, it is symptomatic of social change and is often a source of conflict. As David Reisman* notes in *The Lonely Crowd*, "The current divorce rate is, in part, an index of the new demands made upon marriage for sociability and leisure by sensitive middle-class couples—these demands . . . include the expectation that each partner grow and develop at approximately the same rate as [the other]."

J. M. Mackintosh,† in his essay *Changing Attitudes Within the Family*, also attributes the declining size of the family in part to the improving status of women. He writes that "to both husband and wife it became increasingly evident that an unlimited family threw an intolerable burden on the mother". This concern with the welfare of expectant mothers has turned child-bearing into a normal, healthy function instead of a painful, burdensome disease. Today, moreover, the typical pattern is for pregnancies to be concentrated into the first 10 years of marriage and to take place at *planned* intervals. Professor Titmuss,‡ for instance, has estimated that in the eighteen-nineties the average "working-class mother spent about 15 years in a state of pregnancy and in nursing a baby for the first year of its life"; this 15 years has now dropped to 4.

The increased leisure for women resulting from their fewer confinements and also from their eager adoption of various labour-saving devices in the home has given them far more time and opportunity to take up some extra-familial pursuit, in the form of a kind of leisure which covers a broader horizon than the home itself (e.g. the Women's Institute), or paid employment. Myrdal and Klein§ argue that the contemporary housewife, without these outlets, suffers from social isolation: not only because she must remain in the home to look after the children, but also because of the current

* Reisman, D., *The Lonely Crowd*, Yale University Press, New Haven, Conn., 1950.

† From Rolph, C. H. (ed.), *The Human Sum.*

‡ Titmuss, R. M., *Problems of Social Policy*, Allen & Unwin, London, 1950.

§ Myrdal, A., and Klein, V., *Women's Two Roles: Home and Work*, Routledge & Kegan Paul, London, 1956.

middle-class value of "keeping oneself to oneself". Her solitude makes her feel that life is passing her by and she resents the fact that her husband is virtually her only contact with the outside world. This situation, incidentally, provides another potential source of conflict within the family. Myrdal and Klein further quote from David Reisman's *The Lonely Crowd*: "The housewife, although producing a social work-product, does not find her work explicitly defined . . . in the national census or in people's minds. And since her work is not defined as work, she is exhausted at the end of the day without feeling any right to be." And so, failing to find fulfilment in housewifery alone, the married woman naturally seeks it elsewhere.

In 1951, out of a total labour force in this country of 22½ million, about one-third were women. Of this number, the portion of

TABLE 5

Marital status	Percentage of total number of women at work		
	1921	1931	1951
Single	78	77	54
Married	13	16	38
Widowed and/or divorced	9	7	8

married women had risen steadily since 1921. In the same period, the percentage of all married women who went to work had doubled —from 9 to 21 per cent, and this general trend seems to be characteristic of most Western countries (in the U.S.A., for example, 27 per cent of the labour force are married women). According to estimates by the Ministry of Labour quoted in P. Jephcott's *Married Women Working*,* married women now constitute over half the total of females at work; and some interesting results are obtained if the figures are broken down into age groups. Among married women aged between 25 and 34, two-thirds are in gainful employment of some kind. In the group aged between 35 and 44, the proportion is

* Jephcott, P., Seear, N., and Smith, J., *op. cit.*

three-quarters, dropping to slightly more than two-thirds in the 45–54 grade. Even among women in their early twenties—the group in which one might expect to find the greatest number of mothers with really young children—wives make up more than a third of those at work.

With regard to the types of work most commonly undertaken by women, it appears that nearly half of them work in industry while the rest are engaged in distributive trades and services of all kinds, including insurance, banking, transport, catering and laundries. Some of these tertiary industries are, indeed, predominantly female (such as hairdressing, domestic service, nursing and other medical services). Dr. Lockwood* speaks of the "white-blouse" brigade, those 31 per cent of employed women who work as clerks, typists and shop assistants. Although women are frequently engaged in non-manual jobs, there are also some manufacturing industries which rely on large quantities of female labour. Examples include clothing and textiles, or the manufacture of electric lamps and radio valves (in which women are able to use to advantage their greater manual dexterity). In some large industries, such as those connected with food, the proportion of women employed may be as high as 40 per cent. In engineering, on the other hand, women comprise no more than a quarter of the total, and these are concentrated in light engineering. As Zweig† points out, women tend to congregate in particular branches of industry, like clothing and toy manufacture, because these are occupations which have traditionally been performed by women. When the Industrial Revolution took these processes out of the home and into the factory, women have been willing to follow the trend.

Undoubtedly one of the most potent factors encouraging firms to take on women in recent years has been the general situation of over-employment existing in most sectors of industry since the war. The exigencies first of reconstruction and then of rearmament, plus the tendency of young people to undertake longer periods of further

* Lockwood, D., *The Black-Coated Worker*, Allen & Unwin, London, 1958.

† Zweig, F., *op. cit.*

education, plus the increase in the number of old people in the population, produced a gap in the supply of labour, relative to the demand, which women were called upon to fill. Once virtually all the unmarried women had been employed, any further increase could only come from married women. Their return to work was made possible, as has already been suggested, by the smaller size of the family and by the practice of concentrating procreation and child-rearing in the first 10 to 15 years of marriage. It is interesting to note that firms now show a far greater willingness to employ married women, although more has to be spent on keeping the factory attractive and on welfare services.

The reasons which prompt married women to seek employment are many and varied, but of course the most obvious is the desire for more money. That this may not be the predominant causal factor has been shown by various psychological studies of motivation, and also by Zweig, although his research illustrates how difficult it is accurately to establish motives. When asked why they went to work, his subjects may have been ashamed to admit that they needed the money, and may have therefore expressed some other reason. Be that as it may, it is still true that economic factors do drive a large number of married women into paid employment. What is the money used for? Not for the provision of basic needs, since Zweig's sample of working wives, although small, did show that very few cases could be described as unsatisfactory in terms of the housekeeping allowance provided by the husband—eighteen out of a total of ninety-two, to be exact. Zweig asserts, on the basis of his general experience, that no more than a third of the total of married women at work are in jobs because their housekeeping money is inadequate or non-existent. The majority, he suggests, go to work to provide "extras" for all the family and for the house.

This view is supported by P. Jephcott's *Married Women Working*,* which indicates the common patterns of expenditure: better furniture, house decorations, clothes (for the children rather than the parents), more expensive food, holidays, or capital outlays such as a TV set or a car. In this connection, an important post-war trend has

* Jephcott, P., Seear, N., and Smith, J., *op. cit.*

been the influence of the new towns and housing estates. Young and Willmott* show that people in these new areas depend on "conspicuous consumption", a phrase coined by Veblen,† in order to establish their status, and the wives consequently must go out to work to keep up the hire purchase payments.

A further factor, arising out of the above, is that when families make the sudden transition from an old-established neighbourhood with a strong social life to a virgin housing estate, they may experience a good deal of loneliness, at least initially. The wives, in particular, may miss the gossip and chatter of the streets, and seek a substitute in the companionship of the office or factory.

Thirdly, married women nowadays have far more time on their hands. Not only does the modern woman have fewer children than her grandmother, but her years of active child-rearing are over earlier. Professor Titmuss‡ points out that

> by the time the full cycle of child care had run its course the mother [i.e. of 50 years ago] had only a few more years to live. . . . The typical working-class mother in the industrial towns in 1900 could expect, if she survived to fifty-five, to live not much more than another twelve years. . . . The situation today is remarkably different . . . most mothers have largely concluded their maternal role by the age of forty. At this age, a woman can now expect to live thirty-six years. . . . What these changes mean is that by the time the typical mother of today has virtually completed the cycle to motherhood she still has practically half her total life expectancy to live.

Added to this are the devices which make housekeeping, if not completely effortless, a good deal less than a full-time occupation. Small wonder that the married woman feels both willing and able to partake in some activity outside the home, whether paid or unpaid. In this connection, it is worth noting that the opposition shown by many middle-class husbands to their wives working is on the decline, though they have never objected to *unpaid* employment, such as the Women's Voluntary Service. This opposition used to be based on the assumption that paid jobs for women are associated with working-

* Young, M., and Willmott, P., *op. cit.*

† Veblen, T., *Theory of the Leisure Class*, London, 1924.

‡ Titmuss, R. M., *Essays on the Welfare State*, Allen & Unwin, London, 1958.

class habits, where wives have to go out to work; but today, although it is true that the working-class wife does seek employment more frequently than her middle-class equivalent, the distinction is not significant. Young families of whatever social origin find it increasingly difficult to establish a home, in the prevailing economic conditions, on the basis of the husband's income alone.

Once at work, women tend to be concentrated in the relatively unskilled jobs, not necessarily because they lack ability but because they are not interested in self-advancement. They regard industry as a man's world and they enter it simply as a means to an end; perhaps for this reason, they are difficult to organize in large numbers. Very few will join a trades union, and those who do will invariably be passive members; they develop little sense of comradeship and "belongingness" in the firm, and no interest at all in such matters as joint consultation. On the other hand, women possess a greater sense of loyalty towards their employers and will obey orders more readily than male employees. They like routine and are frightened of change, because of what Zweig* calls their "innate conservatism", yet this may be an advantage to a firm which requires them to do simple but repetitive tasks—for which, so it is said, women are admirably suited.

Something has already been said on the question of housekeeping allowances. It is interesting that the unsatisfactory cases, quoted by Zweig, occurred mostly in the elderly or middle-aged categories. The improved situation for younger couples was summed up by an elderly woman, who told Zweig that "Men nowadays take out their wives more frequently than they used to in old times and they pay better housekeeping money. Women nowadays have a better deal than we had in our times." It appears that, for most wives, the housekeeping allowance does not fluctuate from week to week, except for those whose husbands' earnings vary (such as window-cleaners), and even here there is a tendency for the allowance to be stabilized. If the man gets a rise, it is customary for the wife to receive only a proportionate increase. The weekly amount of the housekeeping money is almost invariably based only on the husband's

* Zweig, F., *op. cit.*

regular wage, excluding overtime and bonus earnings. With the growing egalitarianism in marriage, it is becoming very rare to find marriages where either partner has sole, undisputed control over the family finances. Typically, such matters are now the mutual concern of husband and wife.

It is clear that part of the conflict, between motherhood and a career, is artificial, since there is little evidence to support the pessimists' beliefs* that the employment of wives contributes to delinquency and neglect of children. The Bermondsey report† showed that children of working mothers, far from suffering ill-effects, did *better* in the eleven-plus examination, became independent and "grown-up" more quickly, were every bit as healthy, and were more regular attenders at school than those with "housewife" mothers. The most striking of the discoveries was in the eleven-plus results. The proportion of children with working mothers declined sharply the "lower" the status of school for which they were selected —grammar, technical, comprehensive and secondary modern. For confirmation about the child's behaviour at school, forty-two Bermondsey head-teachers were asked for their opinion: twenty generally approved of working mothers, fifteen had some reservations, and only seven were strongly opposed. As regards the children's own views, Pearl Jephcott says: "They often enjoy their improved status: it feels grown-up to have the key, the run of the home and the chance to boss the younger ones about." From the point of view of the national economy, too, the advantages of employing married women are tremendous: allowing for an average marriage age of 25 (actually a little above the norm) and a 15-year period for child-rearing, there are 20 years left before the normal retiring age of 60. If wives could be persuaded to devote at least

* For example, in a House of Lords debate on women in industry (June 1963), the Bishop of Lichfield built up a bleak picture of children who "returned home from school to an empty house, with a grate in which are the burnt-out remains of a fire and on the table the unwashed breakfast things". He said it conflicted with the "natural order of things". Perhaps more pertinently, Lord Amwell argued that it was against socialist principles for husbands to help with the domestic chores if their wives went out to work!

† Jephcott, P., Seear, N., and Smith, J., *op. cit.*

some of this time to paid employment, the increase in the labour force (and the corresponding increase in the production and supply of goods) would be vastly worthwhile.*

MARRIAGE AND DIVORCE

Christianity, based on the doctrines of St. Paul, has always stressed the indissolubility of marriage, and its loathing of adultery is incorporated in the Ten Commandments. There were several loopholes in this regulation against divorce in the medieval period, and it was not until the Council of Trent (1545) that divorce was finally abolished. The Roman Catholic Church, however, has always provided one way out in the form of the Decree of Nullity, whereby a marriage may be declared null and void after an inquiry by an ecclesiastical court. Although this is not exactly equivalent to a divorce, it is more frequently used than is generally imagined. The

* The case is overwhelmingly argued in Myrdal, A., and Klein, V., *Women's Two Rules: Home and Work* (Routledge & Kegan Paul, London, 1956) and more information may be obtained from Yudkin, S., and Holme, A., *Working Mothers and Their Children* (Michael Joseph, London, 1963), which points out the striking fact that even in 1851 there were 2,500,000 full-time working women. Indeed, the proportion of women at work in 1881 was only 1·7 per cent lower than in 1951, although these statistics alone do not show that the motives for going to work are now entirely different from those operative in the nineteenth century. This survey of 1209 mothers showed that about half did full-time work, mostly in shops and factories; of those doing part-time work, the majority was employed in shops and domestic work. Only 198 gave non-economic reasons for going out to work, such as desire for companionship or an interesting job. About as many again were driven out by genuine necessity. For most the motive was to improve the family's standard of living. Arrangements for the children included relations, neighbours and older children, rather than public facilities such as nursery schools. As regards the effects on the children themselves, the authors conclude that up to the age of 3, a child without its mother can do well only if it adopts someone else as a mother-figure—and so, inevitably, the true mother is the loser. Between 3 and 5, the child positively benefits from some hours a day away from her, provided that it gets enough "loving attention" from whoever is in charge. Once the child is at school, everything hinges on what happens after school and in the holidays; hence only the "latch-key children" suffer. The rather obvious conclusion to be drawn from this is that the mere fact of the mother working is not significant; what is important is the care arranged for her children in her absence. See also Klein, V., *Working Wives*, Institute of Personnel Management, London, 1960.

Sacred Roman Rota, the final court of appeal, deals now with about 200 cases a year, granting nullity to about half. The Church of England is far more tolerant, even allowing individual clergy, if they wish, to perform a marriage for a divorced person with a spouse still living. Few actually do, but the fact remains that the permission is there.

So far as civil divorce is concerned, this was obtainable only by private Act of Parliament until 1857, when the Divorce Court was set up, and even then it was clearly only available to the wealthy. In 1925 a first attempt was made to give assistance to poorer people requiring a divorce, and this achievement was consolidated by the 1949 Legal Aid Act. Today, the average divorce suit costs about £100, but it may cost much less, or even nothing at all, to anyone who can satisfy the Legal Aid Committee that he has a prima facie case and limited means.

Current divorce law has been much criticized because it is still based on the principle of the matrimonial offence. In order to secure a divorce, it must be shown that a "guilty" spouse has committed a matrimonial offence (in practice, adultery, desertion or cruelty) against an "innocent" spouse. If the husband is the "guilty" partner, he must support his ex-wife; if the wife is "guilty", she must support herself. Unfortunately, the retention of the matrimonial offence excludes the most straightforward reason why marriages break down: because the partners can no longer get on with each other. What little evidence there is suggests that couples do not seek divorces because one of the spouses commits a matrimonial offence, but simply because they cannot make their marriages work. For example, it can be logically shown that if people were taking marriage more lightly and divorce more easily, then it would be expected that the divorce rate for recent marriages would rise. This is not borne out by the facts, as Table 6 indicates. Also, the fact that 60 per cent of divorces occur among couples whose marriages have lasted more than 10 years does not suggest an enthusiasm for trivial marriages.

No one can deny that there has been an increase in the number of divorces since the beginning of this century. However, it is not necessarily correct to infer from this that the incidence of broken

TABLE 6

Divorce petitions in years of marriage	Total Divorces (%)	
	1899–1903	1951–4
1–5	14·7	9·9
20 or more	12·4	20·7

marriages has also been increasing. The Report of the Royal Commission on Marriage and Divorce* concludes that "matrimony is not so secure now as it was a hundred or even fifty years ago. . . There is a tendency to take the duties and responsibilities of marriag. less seriously than formerly . . . its growth is insidious and endangere the whole stability of marriage." Is there any truth in this pictures

First, this century's divorce trends can be clearly shown in Table 7,

TABLE 7

Year(s)	Average number of divorce petitions per year
1901–5	810
1911–15	1,030
1921–5	2,850
1931–5	4,780
1941–5	16,070
1946–50	38,900
1951–5	32,170
1956–60	27,480
1961	31,900

which indicates that in terms of divorce petitions alone, the number of broken marriages has risen from 700 in 1906 to 31,900 in 1961. The figure of 38,900 divorces for the period 1946–50 is an average *annual* rate, and conceals the fact that in 1947 the number of decrees absolute granted reached its post-war peak at just over 60,000; since that year, the numbers have significantly declined. Furthermore, it should be remembered that not all divorce petitions are successful:

* Royal Commission on Marriage and Divorce: *Report* (Cmd. 9678), 1956.

in 1961, for instance, 26,360 decrees absolute were granted (albeit the highest figure for 6 years).

The next question concerns the number of divorces as a proportion of the total number of marriages, and here again there is some support for the Royal Commission's assertion. The figures reveal (Table 8) that the number of marriages likely to end in divorce has

TABLE 8

Year	Divorces as a percentage of the total number of marriages
1911	0·2
1921	0·8
1937	1·6
1950	7·1
1953	7·0
1954	6·7

risen from 0·2 per cent in 1911 to about 7 per cent at the present time. Yet even this immense increase still only affects a small section of the married population. It is of course equally true that 93 out of every 100 marriages do not end in divorce; and of the seven that do, four will be replaced by new marriages contracted by the divorced parties. We are still very far from the situation in the U.S.A., where one in four marriages ends in divorce, and where a State like California can have 42,000 marriages a year and 39,000 divorces. Despite the fact that 55 per cent of these divorces are people who enter California from States with stricter laws, those figures are still alarming.

But in both this country and the U.S.A., the divorce rate alone cannot be used as an index of broken homes, for, in the words of O. R. McGregor, "there is no evidence that a higher proportion of marriages break up today than fifty years ago, although there has been a massive increase in de jure dissolutions of marriages already broken de facto." The argument is that in the past there must have been many more concealed broken marriages, due to the financial inability of the partners to enter into divorce proceedings. The introduction of legal aid has merely made divorce available to the masses. Indeed, recent investigations have shown that a manual worker (or his wife) is now statistically as likely as his employer (or his wife) to petition for divorce. Apart from monetary considerations, potential divorce cases at the turn of the century must have been deterred, to a large extent, by the social stigma attached to divorce. This has since become less important, although a divorced person is still not permitted to marry into the Royal Family.

In 1900 only the well-off could afford access to the High Court, with its power to remedy matrimonial difficulties by dissolving marriages. The majority (and this accounts for more than 90 per cent of the marriage breakdowns in that period) had to be content with proceedings in magistrates courts, which enabled poor women to live separately from their husbands, but preserved the marriage bonds intact. At the turn of the century, about 7500 maintenance orders were being granted annually to married women; husbands can apply for separation orders, but cannot obtain maintenance orders against their wives. This figure had risen to 14,489 in 1951–4. However, it is not known how many maintenance orders have been rescinded *de facto* by the return of a wife to her husband, or *de jure* by application to the court. The figures must therefore be interpreted with caution and allowance made for the unknown proportion of "dead" orders.

Nevertheless, it is clear that, while there has been an *absolute* increase in the number of divorces, it is manifestly wrong to speak of a *continuing* increase. On the contrary, the rise can always be associated with the effects of particular events, such as the Poor Persons' Procedure Act of 1925, the Matrimonial Causes Act of 1937 (which extended the justification for divorce to cover such reasons as mental cruelty), the Legal Aid Act of 1949, etc. Rowntree and Carrier* point out that the main increases in the divorce rate have always occurred immediately after outbreaks of war: 1919 and 1947 respectively mark the peaks for the years after World Wars I

* Rowntree, G., and Carrier, N., "The Resort to Divorce in England and Wales, 1858–1957", *Population Studies*, xi, 3, March 1958.

and II. Since about 1952 the incidence of divorce has remained fairly steady (indeed, until 1957 there was a slow decline), and the rise in 1961 does not necessarily presage a long-term trend.

What are the potential causes of divorce? Some have already been mentioned, including the fact that divorce, like education, has now been made available to all sections of society. As the last paragraph indicates, many of this century's increases in the divorce rate can be traced almost directly to the periodic introduction of new avenues of escape from an unsuccessful marriage. The effects of war were most important in this respect and, in the immediate post-war years, there were special facilities for servicemen and their wives to obtain divorces. Long periods of separation for married couples during the war imposed a great strain on wives in particular, and this easily accounts for the astronomical divorce figures in 1947.

The basic factors behind most contemporary marriage failures are more complex and more difficult to unravel. I think the most significant element, however, is the egalitarianism which characterizes the relationship between married partners today, by contrast with the patriarchal authoritarianism which was accepted as the normal pattern in the nineteenth century. In the words of a psychiatrist,* "The marriage a girl enters today has far more stresses than her grandmother's. A partnership needs much more forbearance than the situation where the wife just used to accept the idea of doing what she was told." Indeed, the Victorian woman's attitude to marriage was not one of great enthusiasm even at the outset, since she knew that it was only the prelude to an interminable period of child-care and constant subordination. Although many women accepted this stoically as their lot, some eventually rebelled, with the result that women today enjoy a far higher standard of personal freedom than at any earlier period of history.

Writers differ on the number, and degree of importance, of stresses which beset the contemporary family's existence. It may be true that a marriage could break down through the inability of the partners to attain an ideal relation of equal partnership. On the other

* Quoted by Cooper, S., "Till Divorce Us Do Part", *Sunday Times*, 11 and 18 November 1962.

hand, Willmott and Young* argue that the egalitarian marriage, in most cases, produces far greater happiness and security in the family as a whole:

> . . . the younger husband of today does not consider that the children belong exclusively to his wife's world, or that he can abandon them to her (and her mother) while he takes his comfort in the male atmosphere of the pub. He now shares the responsibility for the number of children as well as for their welfare after they are born. . . . The man's earnings may still be his affair, but when it comes to the spending of the money, his part of the wages as well as hers, husband and wife will share the responsibility. . . . Not only do fathers, as well as mothers, have more money; they also take a pride in their children's turn-out. Both of them now share in the hopes and plans for their children's future.

The authors conclude that the old type of family, at least in the working class, is dead, replaced by "a new kind of companionship between man and woman, reflecting the rise in status of the young wife and children which is one of the great transformations of our time."

The second basic element in many divorces is paradoxically the fact that marriages are lasting longer. There has been a general increase in life expectations, so that marriages which terminated in the cemetery in 1900 now survive to be terminated in the divorce court. Also, couples are getting married younger, thereby exposing themselves to matrimonial risks for longer periods. It has already been shown that a woman at the age of 40 has almost half her life-span in front of her and has already reared all the planned children of her first marriage. The 1960 statistics reveal that, if remarriage is the triumph of hope over experience, nearly 72,000 optimists went to the altar or the register office in that year, and of these almost exactly half were divorced men or women.

Similarly, 1960 also indicates the increasing popularity of marriage among younger people. From a total of 343,614 marriages in England and Wales, more than a third of the brides, and 11·7 per cent of the bridegrooms, were minors† (the overall average marriage

* Young, M., and Willmott, P., *op. cit.*

† The Registrar-General's *Statistical Review for England and Wales, 1961* (H.M.S.O., London, 1963) illustrates these points to an even greater degree. Of a total of 346,678 marriages, there were 6247 brides aged 16. For every four marriages in 1960 where both bride and groom were under 20, there

age for girls was 23·3 years, for men 26·7 years). The correlation between earlier marriages and the risk of divorce can be shown by the fact that, among couples separated in 1959, after remaining together for between 4 and 11 years, the rate for those where the wife had been under 20 on the wedding day was almost four times as high as the rate for the group as a whole. Another significant point concerns the large number of marriages where the bride was pregnant on her wedding day. In 1960, nearly 62,000 extra-maritally conceived children were born to women married for less than 8 months (usually 5 or 6). Translated into a proportion of all marriages, this means that one in five brides was pregnant, and it is well established that the shot-gun marriage is more likely to break down.

Some of the so-called threats to the unity of the family are more hypothetical. M. Penelope Hall,* for instance, refers to the growth of the factory system, which has made the individual wage-earner the economic unit of society, rather than the family group. Yet was it really desirable that all members of the family should be forced, from the earliest age, to labour at home in the most depressing, insanitary and overcrowded conditions? In the words of one commissioner quoted in the Hand-Loom Weavers Report† of 1840, "domestic happiness is not promoted but impaired by all the members of a family muddling together and jostling each other constantly in the same room".

Another potentially disruptive influence mentioned by M. Penelope Hall is that improved contraceptive techniques have affected the biological basis of family life by removing "the age-old connection between sexual intercourse and child-bearing and rearing". Enough has already been said about women's new-found freedom from premature death brought about by constant pregnancies. Although sexual incompatibility may be responsible for some marriage breakdowns, the attainment of a successful partnership in this field, for most people, is a bond uniting man and wife even closer together.

---

were nearly five in 1961, and the most common age for marriage had become 22 for men, 21 for women.

* Hall, M. P., *op. cit.*

† Quoted in Fletcher, R., *op. cit.*

One most important aspect of divorce concerns the treatment of the children who are the innocent victims of the marriage breakdown. About 17,000 children annually are affected by their parents' divorces. It is well established that the children of separated parents have an above-average chance of themselves ending with divorce, possibly because such children grow up without adequate emotional security.* On the other hand, while no one would wish to underestimate the amount of suffering experienced by the children of broken homes, it is too easy to exaggerate the problem. First, one must bear in mind the slight tendency of the overall divorce rate to decline, coupled with the fact that by the time many marriages reach the divorce court the children are either fairly mature or completely adult—they will certainly not be dependent infants. Second, the vast majority of divorces occurs among childless couples or those with only one child. In the words of the *Statistical Review* of 1957,† "divorce rates among childless couples may be something like twice as high as the average for the marriage age-group concerned, perhaps not quite so much in the oldest groups". The figures in Table 9

TABLE 9

	Average annual percentage of divorce petitions, by number of children	
	0	1
1899–1903	40	24
1951–4	33	33

point to a fairly consistent situation in this century, namely that about two-thirds of all divorces occur in couples with either no children or a single offspring. By contrast, only 7 per cent of broken

* According to one person who, as a child, had been in this situation: "By the time I was eighteen I felt like a parcel in the post, not really belonging anywhere." (Quoted in Cooper, S., "Till Divorce Us Do Part", *Sunday Times*, 18 November 1962.)

† Registrar-General's *Statistical Review for England and Wales, 1957*, H.M.S.O., London.

marriages in 1957 involved families with four or more children. Indeed, it seems accurate to infer that divorce rates are highest for childless couples, and gradually decline in proportion to increasing family size.

CONCLUSION

From the material in this chapter, it must now be clear that, far from being in moral, physical and functional decline, the family today is simply undergoing a process of change, whereby it is being adjusted to meet the demands of a highly complex industrial society. The fact that so much literature is devoted to the family surely indicates that its importance is being recognized as never before. Professor Titmuss* writes:

> the family of today is a social institution. The health and stability of the community is now seen to rest on the health and stability of its families; the social health of the individual personality is now judged to depend in great measure upon the quality of parent-child relationships. These are accepted generalities today; fifty years ago they were not.

The emancipation of women, shorter working hours and increased opportunities for leisure, social welfare, new attitudes to children and family planning—all these factors, and more, have turned the modern family into an institution vastly different from its Victorian forebears. Indeed, so great is the difference that it is perhaps pointless to attempt comparisons between the two periods, but it is clear that the standards demanded of marriage have been raised. The need for companionship is today a requirement accepted by the family members; there is more introspection about personal relationships and compatibility. It is not therefore surprising that more people turn to divorce as a way out of their apparently insoluble problems: in short, the current divorce rates do not necessarily mean that there are more unhappy marriages, but that more couples than ever before are willing *publicly* to terminate their marriages, instead of allowing the *de facto* break to remain hidden.

* Titmuss, R. M., *The Family*, National Council of Social Service.

In Ronald Fletcher's* words: "In spite of the problems brought about through change, the picture of marriage in modern Britain is, surely, a picture of considerable health, considerable stability, and an enlarged degree of opportunity and happiness."

* Fletcher, R., *op. cit.*

Social Cl. Registrar Gen. Figures for 1960.
16 Socio-Economic Groups

1. Prof occupn.
2. Int. occupns.
3 Skilled
4. Partly skilled
5 Unskilled

CHAPTER 3

The Class Structure

During a pre-election survey I found that all working-class families I approached were not concerned with a summit meeting or Nyasaland but only with making their homes warmer, snugger, tighter, more secluded and private.

(DR. MARK ABRAMS *at B.I.M. Conference, Harrogate,* 1959.)

The poorest he that is in England has a life to live as the greatest he.

(COLONEL RAINBOROUGH.)

THE WORKING CLASS

The initial problem, as usual, is one of definition, since the word "class" itself is subject to many interpretations. Clearly what is implied here is a certain stratum in society which, according to the evaluation of the majority of people, carries the lowest prestige.

Income has been suggested as one criterion for determining social class, the recipients being graded according to the size of their income, irrespective of how it has been earned. Those within the lower ranges are said to constitute the working class. This holds good to a certain extent, but income *per se* is not a satisfactory principle for establishing class, if only because, as Lockwood* describes, the question of occupational prestige interferes with simple economic gradations. Manual work is generally considered as possessing lower status than non-manual work, yet many occupations within the skilled manual range receive higher wages than the lesser clerical jobs. Curates, for example, earn less than dock labourers. Moreover,

* Lockwood, D., *The Blackcoated Worker*, Allen & Unwin, London, 1958.

how can celebrities such as pop-singers be assigned their correct class position, when they undoubtedly fall into one of the highest income categories?

The difficulties of using income as a criterion of class are increased by the incidence of graded taxation and death duties, which reduce inequalities in the distribution of income; these topics are analysed in greater detail later in the chapter. Whereas the overall national income in recent years has doubled, the lower income group's share of it has trebled, due partly to the onset of the Welfare State ideology, and partly to this group's own efforts for wage increases. The range between the highest and lowest incomes may still be very great, but the income gap between the middle and working classes has been significantly reduced. This has enabled the gap to be narrowed in other ways. Willmott and Young,* for example, writing of Bethnal Green, refer to the attitude, once exclusively middle-class, of deciding *beforehand* the number of children to be had, on the basis of what the family could afford. Clearly this trend towards income equality is having a levelling effect in at least some respects. Perhaps most striking is the degree of standardization within the working class itself, as the wages of unskilled and semi-skilled workers approximate more closely with those of skilled employees.

Income is often associated with two other factors: relationship to the means of production, and security of employment. Together, these constitute the Marxian economic approach to class. When Marx wrote, they were probably the most efficient criteria for establishing the working class, which was characterized by small, inadequate incomes and the necessity for selling its labour to those who owned the means of production. Today, by contrast, trade unions do much to increase the job-security of their members, and it has been frequently demonstrated, in recent years, how the traditional security of the white-collar worker is by no means as assured as it once was. The 1952 National Advisory Committee, in fact, reported that it is the managerial, clerical and unskilled workers who have the greatest difficulty in becoming re-employed in a depression. Yet

* Young, M., and Willmott, P., *Family and Kinship in East London*, Routledge & Kegan Paul, London, 1957.

they are emphatically not a homogeneous class group because of this common dilemma alone. Insecurity is further reduced nowadays by the fact that both main political parties guarantee full employment as a basic principle of their official policies. Relationship to the means of production is now considered a rather meaningless criterion of class, as the vast majority of people make their living by selling their labour. This majority includes, for example, the professions, who are clearly not considered as members of the working class in the accepted sense of the term.

The most popular and frequently used determinant of class is, of course, occupation. It is considered the best criterion because it is highly correlated with size of income, it helps shape the way of life and it is firmly associated with social prestige. Generally the distinction is made between manual and non-manual workers, with the former subdivided into skilled, semi-skilled and unskilled categories. Zweig* describes what is usually meant by the working class in terms of occupation. First comes the bottom layer of unemployables, their condition being attributable to disablement, mental or physical defects, ill-health or age. Then the labourers—heavy, general and light labourers, craftsmen's labourers and handymen—followed by the semi-skilled men, a group which is steadily increasing its numbers with the mechanization of industry; this category consists essentially of machine operators. Finally Zweig refers to the class of craftsmen and skilled men, leading to the supervisory grades of leading hands, chargehands, sub-foremen and foremen.

In 1950 Hall and Caradog Jones reported the first English study of occupational prestige. The question under review was whether the general public ranked occupations in trades similar to those of the standard classification. In the event no significant variations were found. On the other hand, this single survey cannot be said to have decided the problem once and for all, since Young and Willmott's inquiry into Bethnal Green revealed a significant deviant group which graded occupations according to their usefulness to society,

* Zweig, F., *The British Worker*, Penguin Books; see also, Zweig, F., *The Worker in an Affluent Society*, Heinemann, London, 1961.

manual workers being ranked *above* non-manual workers on the whole. Occupation as a determinant of social grading is only successful, therefore, up to a point. Status ambiguity occurs especially among those occupations where the size of the income has not kept up with the prestige usually accorded to the job. Lockwood,* for instance, shows that until the last two decades the mass of clerical workers had been better off in income terms than the mass of manual workers. Today this is no longer true. It remains to be seen whether the old occupational prestige associated with white-collar work, as opposed to manual work, will hold out against lower relative incomes, loss of the monopoly of literacy, declining responsibilities, etc. It is interesting to note, moreover, that although manual workers are more likely to allocate high prestige to manual jobs (such as agricultural labourer, coal-miner, bricklayer), they are also enthusiastic that their children should obtain the best education possible. Presumably this is because they view education as a means to an end—the end being the "better" job, for which educational qualifications are essential. Such jobs are almost invariably non-manual.

Another way of isolating the working class is by subjective assessment, the class being said to consist of those who consider themselves as members. Much is said of working-class solidarity and their strong sense of positive partnership in a cohesive group. Hoggart† speaks of the common feeling of all being in the same boat together, the neighbourliness, the attachment to home and family, the friendship, the hedonistic ability to enjoy oneself in the present instead of postponing satisfactions. He also speaks of the pressures to conform, of the partial isolation of those who achieve grammar school education, of the dislike of snobbery and the Queen's English. But, supposing that a class exists such as Hoggart describes, who are the people who consider themselves to belong to it?

Martin's study‡ shows the possible results when a stratified sample of subjects, graded according to the Hall-Jones objective

* Lockwood, D., *op. cit.*

† Hoggart, R., *The Uses of Literacy*, Chatto & Windus, London, 1957.

‡ Martin, F. M., in Glass, D. V. (Ed.), *Social Mobility in Britain*, Routledge & Kegan Paul, London, 1954.

classification, is asked to grade itself. The nearest approach to unanimity between objective and subjective status was found in the extreme groups of very rich and very poor. On the other hand, one-quarter of manual workers assigned themselves to the middle class and one-quarter of black-coated workers assigned themselves to the working class. Willmott and Young's survey of Woodford* threw this question into even greater relief. Asked which class they thought they belonged to, nearly half (48 per cent) of the 355 manual workers in the general sample considered themselves middle class. Identification with the middle class was nearly as common among unskilled and semi-skilled workers as among skilled employees. Of the 257 skilled workers in the general sample, 49 per cent said they were middle class (either upper, middle, or lower middle); of the 98 semi-skilled and unskilled, the equivalent proportion was 43 per cent. Apparently Woodford was not unusual in having manual workers who put themselves into the middle class, but it does have an unusually high proportion who do so. According to the authors, "The rule seems to be that the more the middle class predominates in a district the more working-class people identify themselves with it."

The drawback of accepting this subjective stratification lies in the difficulty of proving that the concepts of working class and middle class mean the same thing to different people. The middle-class deviants who assign themselves to the working class may think of the middle classes as reserved specifically for the professions and the working classes as composed of all those who are paid wages or salaries.

The idea of subjective as opposed to objective class is closely linked with the voting behaviour of the classes. Although this will be covered in more detail in a later chapter, we may say in the present context that one would expect the working class to vote Labour, since this is theoretically the party most likely to further their own interests. C. A. R. Crosland† goes so far as to say that if the working

* Young, M., and Willmott, P., *Family and Class in a London Suburb*, Routledge & Kegan Paul, London, 1960.

† Crosland, C. A. R., *The Future of Socialism*, Cape, London, 1956.

class vote Conservative, they are motivated by one of three situations. First, they do not know where their true interests lie; or second, they know but nevertheless act irrationally; or third they know but are rationally influenced by factors unconnected with class. Zweig,* on the other hand, describes the traditional Socialism of the British workers as "more of a negative attitude against capitalism than a positive attitude towards Socialism", and an "instinctive urge to better the conditions of working men against those in command of them".

In 1950 Birch and Campbell† found that out of a Lancashire sample there was a strong correlation between objective social class and voting behaviour. Benney, Gray and Pear, however, in their book *How People Vote*,‡ found from a Greenwich sample that at first sight subjective class membership appears to show a much stronger relationship with voting than does objective class position. These results may be partly due to the inadequacies of the objective, occupational index of class positions. However, subjective views of class are still of great help in predicting the vote of the border-line cases, whose income and occupation are on the dividing line between the middle and working classes.

Any attempts to stratify classes according to political party *affiliation* (as distinct from voting) are not likely to be successful, for apart from the expected number of deviants, the differences between the parties are getting progressively less. Both have policies of full employment, and both support the Welfare State.

Some authorities consider that style of life is the ultimate factor in deciding social class, that classes are determined by characteristic spending habits, and characteristic ways of spending leisure. As for the former, the working class is considered to spend more on food and less on conspicuous consumption, such as clothes and furnishings, cars and refrigerators. Zweig describes the common attitude to saving as very different from that of the middle classes.

* Zweig, F., *op. cit.*

† Birch, A. H., and Campbell, P., "Voting Behaviour in a Lancashire Constituency", *Brit. J. Sociol.*, September 1950.

‡ Benney, M., Gray, A. P., and Pear, R. H., *How People Vote: A Study of Electoral Behaviour in Greenwich*, Routledge & Kegan Paul, London, 1956.

Saving is condemned as anti-social and indicative of the saver's "black-leg" attempts to climb out of his ordained social group. It is only accepted when it is specifically for holidays; getting married; wishing to buy clothes or Christmas presents.

But class-oriented patterns of consumption are being modified, so much so that Zweig* himself admits that "in a Sunday crowd you can hardly distinguish the working classes from the middle classes, especially in the age-group between 20 and 30". Hire purchase, for example, permits much greater expenditure on conspicuous consumption without interfering with the anti-saving ideology. From September 1958 to April 1960 the total hire purchase debt in this country rose from £481 million to £920 million. In 1959, the highest year so far, total hire purchase sales amounted to £1070 million. Table 10,† prepared by the Odhams Press Research Department, shows what percentage of appliances, sold over the 5 years 1956–60, through hire purchase, went to the different social classes.

TABLE 10

Items	Well-to-do	Junior administrative and clerical workers	Skilled and unskilled workers	Those with £250 p.a. or less
Vacuum cleaner	9	20	69	2
Washing machine	12	18	68	2
TV set	10	16	70	4
Refrigerator	21	27	51	1

There seems little doubt that hire purchase tends to blur class distinctions. The Woodford inquiry‡ showed the reason for the working-class members' claims to middle-class status to lie in their predilection for judging themselves on what they bought, rather than on how they earned their money. Certainly there was the rivalry over possessions and status symbols which now seem to be an essen-

* Zweig, F., *op. cit.*
† Reprinted in the *Observer*, 4 December 1960.
‡ Young, M., and Willmott, P., *op. cit.*

tial concomitant of class aspirations. One labourer's wife said: "We get a new Hoover, so she's got to have one. Another neighbour's got a new studio couch, so she's got one and she's still paying for it."

Moreover, the traditionally accepted spending habits of the working class are altering. Dr. Mark Abrams* has suggested how the greater prosperity of the working class in World War II was mainly devoted to more beer, cigarettes, and cinemas. In the 1950's the emphasis had changed to food, housing, fuel and light, household goods, private motoring and foreign travel. The biggest jump in spending involved motoring, which showed an increase of 276 per cent between 1948–50 and 1957–9. This was followed by expenditure abroad (63 per cent) and household goods (50 per cent). Whereas people normally spend proportionately less of their incomes on food as their standards of living rise, this has not been true of Britain in recent years. On the contrary, people have been cutting down on the traditional "filler" foods and choosing the more expensive and attractive meat, fresh vegetables, and fruit. As Dr. Abrams remarks: "In the past two or three years it has become clear that young working-class wives are rapidly acquiring many middle-class ideas about meals".

Ways of spending leisure are also thought of as a means of differentiating between social classes. Gambling, drinking and sports of all kinds were once considered the traditional leisure pursuits of the working class: but they cannot be considered to have a monopoly over these particular leisure occupations. Recent years, moreover, have seen a considerable democratization of leisure. Formerly there was a marked difference in the amount and type of leisure between the upper and middle classes and the working class, the latter being characterized by its lack of social amenities—no parks, playing fields, libraries, etc. But after 1850 these began to be provided, working hours were shortened and paid holidays eventually introduced. The great recreational media of the time—the cinema, the popular press, TV and radio—apply almost equally to all classes.

* Speech at British Institute of Management Conference, Harrogate, as reported in *The Times Weekly Review*, 26 November 1959.

For some people, it is the general pattern of family life, the resulting personality formation and inculcation of a common ideology which characterizes the working classes. In talking about the working-class family, however, considerable difficulty is encountered. So many case studies from different areas have been made that the result is to a certain extent confusing, showing that the working class is, if anything, not a homogeneous group. Thus *Coal is Our Life* speaks of a family system in which "husband and wife live separate, and in a sense, secret lives", whereas Willmott and Young's work in the East End* revealed "a living extended family which includes within it three, and even four generations" in which husbands generally play an equal part. However, there are certain basic characteristics. For instance, the family is primarily a functional unit, the home is a place in which to eat and sleep and spend one's leisure if one so wishes. Industrialization has destroyed the home as a unit of production and the family now concentrates on alternative social functions, such as reproduction and the early socialization of children. Yet none of this is exclusively a working-class phenomenon and cannot therefore be cited as a class determinant.

More significant is the fact that in the working classes there appears to be a greater segregation of the sexes, in work, in leisure, in the ideology as to the position of the sexes and in the division of the wage-packet. A man's work is his own concern, while a woman's domain is the house. From an early age, the males move outside the family to a unisexual play-group in the streets. Girls, on the other hand, are expected to have little initiative; their education is often considered a waste of time and their primary concern is getting a husband. According to Hoggart's rather impressionistic account,† there is a phase in their teens when they are allowed to have a good time, but this is not considered the real business of life, which is getting married and having a family. While the head of the family is ostensibly the husband (as the wage-earner), the wife occupies the central position as mother and boss in running the home. There is also a division concerning the wage-packet. In general, the husband

* Young, M., and Willmott, P., *op. cit.*
† Hoggart, R., *op. cit.*

keeps a share as pocket-money and hands over the rest as housekeeping money to the wife; neither inquires how the other spends their share, so long as all is functioning smoothly. Wives are often ignorant of the actual size of the income. This segregation between the sexes is, however, believed to be diminishing. Husbands are becoming more interested in the home, in the upbringing and future of their children, whereas this used to be the exclusive concern of the wife.

Of the many studies, it is difficult to say which is the most representative of the working class, for regional differences are often reported in the functions and attitudes of the family. Dennis, Henriques and Slaughter,* for example, speaking of an obscure mining village in the north of England, strongly emphasize the division between the sexes. In this village, a woman's place is emphatically in the home and married women at work are looked at askance. Husband and wife practically never go out together; there is no joint entertaining in the home; few common interests. Men are brought up to despise anything suggestive of tenderness or affection; women take refuge in romantic magazine stories and films.

Some surveys support the assumption that the working-class family is dominated by the father in his role as wage-earner. Mays† states of Liverpool households that "The home is in certain important respects male-dominated. The husband and father *qua* wage-earner is the economic master who decides how much of the income will go to housekeeping and how much he will keep for his own personal use." Furthermore, many researches into poverty have shown that the wife often does not know how much her husband earns, and that his contributions to the housekeeping do not rise with the number of children. In Glasgow during the war, for instance, Professor Madge‡ found that husbands earning up to 70*s*. 0*d*. started their wives on 78 per cent of their income, rising

* Dennis, N., Henriques, F., and Slaughter, C., *Coal Is Our Life*, Eyre & Spottiswoode, London, 1956.

† Mays, J. B., *Growing Up in the City*, Liverpool University Press, 1954.

‡ Unpublished research, quoted in Sprott, W. J. H., *Human Groups*, Penguin Books, 1958.

to 84 per cent, 86 per cent and 87 per cent with the first, second, and third children, and thereafter not rising at all. In his second survey of York, Rowntree remarked that "Frequently a woman only knows what money her husband gives her, not how much he actually receives". Again the point is made that women had to exist on housekeeping allowances that did not rise with the size of the family. Willmott and Young* even admit that, while these authoritarian relationships may be disappearing in Bethnal Green, the old habits still linger (perhaps inevitably in a community where young couples live close to their parents). If wives were present when the interviewer asked how much the husbands earned, the latter often became visibly embarrassed or gave a suspiciously round figure. According to the stereotyped idea of the working-class family, husbands were also unsympathetic in other ways: they forced unwanted pregnancies on their wives; they were violent or tyrannical when drunk, which was frequently. At the turn of the century, Helen Bosanquet† wrote that "as the children grow older the chances are that the burden of maintaining the family falls entirely upon the mother". Father could easily leave, ignore his responsibilities and live elsewhere "in some of the many shelters and lodging houses in London". As Willmott and Young remark, quoting Bosanquet, such accounts may have given an accurate representation of the picture at the turn of the century, but today they are inappropriate and irrelevant.

Family Life in East London describes a much less forbidding family life, with the emphasis on the extended family and, within this, the especially strong ties between mother, daughter and grandchildren. The mother is the centre of the family and prospective husbands have to learn two roles: of son-in-law as well as husband. This devoted relationship between daughter and mother means that in old age the elderly are not deserted. Townsend‡ reports that studies of the social background of the elderly in institutions shows how surviving children are the greatest single safeguard for indepen-

* Young, M., and Willmott, P., *op. cit.*

† Bosanquet, H., *The Family*, Macmillan, London, 1906.

‡ Townsend, P., *The Family Life of Old People*, Routledge & Kegan Paul, London, 1958.

dence in old age. The extended family is not without its disadvantages, however, since husbands may feel resentment at the wife's attachment to her family of origin and may therefore turn for consolation outside the home. This accounts for the fact that many London social workers—despite the lack of documented evidence—blame Mum for some broken marriages.

Many factors have collaborated to change the working-class family structure. Thus the birth and death rates have fallen, the former fall in particular being due to the emancipation of women and changed attitudes leading to the conscious planning of children. A new egalitarian relationship in the family has meant that wives are not forced to depend on their mothers to the same extent as formerly. Greater financial security has followed upon the political doctrine of full employment, and the reduction of working hours enables the husband to spend more time at home. Housing, for the most part, is no longer overcrowded, dirty and uncomfortable, and because of this there is no longer any need for the husband to migrate to the pub for his pleasure.

In many studies the husband is shown as a rather solitary figure standing on the edge of the circle of affection and family activity which surrounds the mother. An inquiry into Manchester dock workers* suggests a reason for this, namely that before dock labour was regularized the husband was in the home much more. "The children saw a lot of their father" and he "developed a great interest in and high regard for family life". With the introduction of more systematic working hours, the dock workers are "no longer able to keep in close touch with what is happening at home . . . and find it more difficult to maintain their traditional authority in the family". B. M. Spinley† in her study of Paddington discovered a "family constellation of a dominant female figure . . . with the corollary of a weak and probably variable male figure". As with many similar surveys, Spinley's observations can in no sense be categorized as typical of the working class as a whole, especially as she concentrated

* *The Dock Worker*, Liverpool University Press, 1954.

† Spinley, B. M., *The Deprived and the Privileged*, Routledge & Kegan Paul, London, 1953.

specifically on the child-rearing techniques and consequent personality characteristics of the children.

All studies of this kind are interesting, but they have been attacked as portraying anachronisms, remnants of dying sub-cultures not truly representative of the statistically normal working-class family. For example, it has been alleged that the extended family is no longer of vital importance to the working class. Increasing mobility of labour may have forced the working-class family to rely, like the middle classes, on its own nuclear structure. There can be little doubt that Bethnal Green represents a type of community fast disappearing from the social scene. It is being replaced, for good or ill, by the expanding suburbs and the new towns. Although Geoffrey Gorer* indicates that "once English people have got a house, they tend to stay in it", and Mays† writes that "Where the daughter marries she often elects to live within easy calling distance of her own home, and a mile can be thought of as a wide separation"—these and other similar statements may lose their relevance, if the British working class increasingly adopt the features of the middle classes.

Of course, attempts to differentiate the classes may be made on the basis of certain objective criteria connected with the family, such as population data. The differential infant mortality rate differs as much between classes as it did before World War I, if not more so, although there has been a heavy fall in absolute death rates for all classes. Also, the working class tends to have larger families than the middle classes, despite the general decrease in size for both classes. But such criteria are clearly inadequate, particularly in view of the fact that the large size of working-class families is being emulated by the professional income groups.

Altogether, it would appear that the family is not an entirely satisfactory means of class differentiation, especially as there is a move towards its increasing democratization. Divorce, which was once only enjoyed by the rich, is now available to lower income groups through the Legal Aid Act. The State has taken over many

* Gorer, G., *Exploring English Character*, Cresset Press, London, 1955.
† Mays, J. B., *op. cit.*

of the responsibilities previously exercised by middle and working-class families, such as education and health. Indeed, the provision for secondary education for all under the 1944 Education Act has removed one of the most effective determinants of class, namely, the type and duration of education received. Prior to 1944, only a select minority received secondary education, and the working classes were heavily under-represented. Only a very small proportion of working-class boys achieved secondary education through scholarships to open places. The vast majority had to be content with an inadequate period of elementary tuition in poorly-equipped schools. Since the 1944 Act, however, the grammar school has definitely become the chief agent of social selection. With the abolition of fees and a standardized selection process, there is now little means of distinguishing the social classes according to the type of education received—although the working class as a whole is still marginally under-represented. A greater number of children of skilled workers receive a grammar school education, but little difference has been made to educational chances of children of semi-skilled and unskilled workers. Some working-class children still seem to suffer a handicap in their parents' attitudes to education, despite Young and Willmott's generalization that most parents are deeply conscious of the importance of education, if only as a passport to occupational success. Certainly schools no longer have Boots Funds for barefoot children,* since parents now take a pride in their offspring's appearance. Even so, many working-class children are penalized by the fact that they are members of large families. There is consistently less success in the selection tests for children in this category (probably because constant social intercourse with siblings is of less value, educationally, than the close relationships inevitably existing between, say, an only child and his parents). The importance of education, then, lies not in its intrinsic capacity for acting as an index of social class, but rather in its function as a means of gaining occupational prestige.

* According to a letter from Rt. Hon. Harold Wilson, M.P. (*Daily Telegraph*, 6 March 1963), a large number of boys at his elementary school wore clogs. "As for my own shoes, when worn out, my mother sent them to the 'Boots for the Bairns' fund philanthropically run by a Yorkshire Conservative newspaper."

It is clearly becoming very difficult to isolate the working classes according to some satisfactory criterion, particularly as many of the traditionally distinguishing features are no longer as appropriate as they once were. This trend is likely to continue so long as the economic position and status aspirations of the working class continue to approach those of the present middle class, but there will long be isolated enclaves, particularly in the provinces and remoter parts of Britain, where the "old" working class will persist, firmly resisting change.

THE MIDDLE CLASS

> Their assured, curt voices, their proud carriage, their clothes, the similarity of their manners, all show that they belong to a caste and that caste has been successful in the struggle for life. It is called the middle class, but it ought to be called the upper class, for nearly everything is below it. (ARNOLD BENNETT, "The Middle Class," *Essays*, 1909.)

> A SURVEYOR: We have a very dear friend at Woodford Green who's a practising barrister. It never struck us that people might like to know them just because he was a barrister, but when the wife's needlework group had a meeting there, some of the wives were very pleased just because he was a barrister. Some of them were surprised and a bit annoyed at my wife because she just said "Hullo, Joan" to a barrister's wife. (PETER WILLMOTT and MICHAEL YOUNG, *Family and Class in a London Suburb*.)

Class, as we have seen, is an amalgam of a whole range of factors, including income, occupation, accent, spending habits, residence, culture, leisure pursuits, clothes, education, attitudes and relationships with others. To belong to a given class does not mean that an individual must conform with the class norms in *all* of these respects: it is the combined effect which is important. Accurately to define the middle classes in these terms would be difficult and inordinately tedious. A preferable alternative is probably to exclude all those who are not middle class in our society—the remainder will then belong to the group at present under consideration.

Broadly speaking, the term working class refers to a large body of people chiefly characterized in occupational terms by manual jobs (such as coal miners, factory operatives, etc.) plus a substantial number of non-manual workers (such as junior clerks) who may be on the verge of entry into the lower-middle class. At the other end of the scale is the so-called upper class, perhaps no more than 2 per cent of the population, comprising the aristocracy, "society", and a few important families whose common feature is the ownership of land. Since the Industrial Revolution there has been considerable infiltration into the ranks of the upper class by those who were formerly in the senior ranks of the middle classes—indeed, the continued existence of many large estates may have depended on intermarriage with some *nouveau riche* captain of industry—until today it is scarcely possible to draw a line between the two. Equally, it is virtually out of the question to attempt a definitive barrier between the working and the lower-middle classes. However, by adopting these very broad generalizations, it should be possible to isolate the middle classes by excluding the upper and the working classes in society. This would imply that the middle classes constituted about one-third of the total population. Unfortunately, these theoretical estimates do not coincide with the estimates of the people concerned, for we must take into account the subjective aspirations of those who, objectively, belong to the working class (two-thirds of the population). In 1952, for example, the British Institute of Public Opinion conducted a Gallup Poll, in which a sample of adults throughout Great Britain were asked the question: "If you had to say what social class you belong to, which would it be?"* The replies (given in Table 11) indicate that, of those who replied 49 per cent placed themselves in the middle classes and 46 per cent in the working class.

What is especially significant is that the number of people describing themselves as working class had declined appreciably since a similar inquiry carried out in 1946. Clearly a continuing trend of rising wages had enabled many more working-class people to aspire to a middle-class standard of living. If this trend were to be sustained indefinitely, there would undoubtedly be a gradual accumulation of numbers in

* Peter Willmott (*The Evolution of a Community*, Routledge & Kegan Paul, London, 1963) argues, though not in so many words, that this question is meaningless—on the grounds that if one could question whales, no doubt half of them would say they were fish.

TABLE 11

Class label	Percentage of the whole sample
Upper	1
Upper middle	6
Middle	27
Lower middle	16
Working	46
No reply	4

the middle classes at the expense of the working class, but this movement could easily be halted or even reversed by economic events.

The middle classes cannot be differentiated by reference to income alone, however. Even a casual analysis will show that a manual wage-earner may make more money than, say, a school-teacher or a shopkeeper; and when a middle-class individual retires, his income may be drastically reduced but he still retains his social status. Also, the way in which incomes are paid may be important, for it is significant that the proportion of the national income paid in salaries had risen from 12 per cent in 1911 to 26 per cent in 1935. Today, recruitment to the professions and other occupations carrying social prestige is open to all those possessing the required ability, regardless of social origin. Similarly, further education is not now the sole prerogative of those who can afford it. These factors together have increased the scope of recruitment to the middle classes, and at the same time added to the difficulty of analysing the features common to the group.

The ownership of property might alternatively be taken as the basis of middle-class membership, according to the Marxian analysis. Certainly private property is distributed most unevenly throughout the population; for example, the Oxford Savings Survey* showed that only 5 to 7 per cent of all families own stocks and shares. Ownership even within this group is so heavily concentrated that 0·1 per cent, the families with the largest holdings, account for about

* Hill, T. P., *Bull. Inst. Stat.*, May 1955.

20 per cent of the total number of shares in existence. Expressed in terms of individuals, this means that only 3 per cent of the population owns any shares. Of these, the 30 per cent with the largest holdings possess 87 per cent of the total nominal capital issued. Parkinson's study* corroborates this picture by showing that, in 82 of the largest companies in this country, half of the shares are owned by the largest twenty shareholders. Furthermore, of these twenty, the most important five own 40 per cent of the shares. The same impression of extremely high concentration in share ownership can be obtained from the U.S.A. where 2 per cent of all shareholders own more than half the total number of shares.

These conspicuous differences in share ownership are reflected in the ownership of property as a whole. Much property, in the omnibus sense of the term most appropriate here, takes the form of investment in stocks and shares, building societies, insurance companies, local authorities, land, buildings and business premises. Income derived from sources such as these is classified as "unearned" for the purposes of the Inland Revenue authorities. In the 1952–3 financial year, over a third of the income liable for surtax was in this category. As incomes become very large (i.e. above £20,000), so the proportion of unearned income rises. At the other end of the economic spectrum, if we apply the criterion of "Total Net Worth"—liquid assets, securities, property, private businesses, loans, motor-cars—we find that in 1954 one-third of the population had a Total Net Worth of zero, and over half had less than £100.† Samuel Brittan‡ has pointed out that about 0·5 per cent of the adult population "own a quarter of total personal wealth, worth over £50,000 million." Nearly half of this total personal wealth is held by the top 2 per cent owning more than £20,000 each. And in figures published later,§ Brittan showed that, of the total personal wealth in Britain, 38 per cent is owned by 1 per cent of the adult population (see Table 12).

* Parkinson, H., *Ownership of Industry*, Eyre & Spottiswoode, London, 1951.

† Crosland, C. A. R., *The Future of Socialism*, Cape, London, 1956.

‡ Brittan, S., "Tax Wealth, Not Gains", the *Observer*, 8 April 1962.

§ Brittan, S., "Pay As You Own", the *Observer*, 10 March 1963.

TABLE 12

	People	Wealth	Total wealth (in millions)
	262,000	£20,000–£50,000	£8,400
	70,000	£50,000–£100,000	£5,000
	24,000	£100,000–£200,000	£3,500
	8,000	over £200,000	£4,600
Totals	364,000	over £20,000	£21,500

What of the distribution of incomes? Incomes from labour take the form of wages and salaries, and incomes from investment take the form of rent, interest and profits. Some analysis of the national income may be attempted on this basis—G. D. H. Cole* has estimated that wages and salaries together make up about two-thirds of all income, with self-employed and investment incomes obtaining 11 per cent each—but the figures cannot be very precisely calculated. Professor Titmuss† has shown how official statistics, which theoretically show a continuous trend towards equality of incomes since 1938, can be misleading. By manipulation of his spending power, the individual can minimize his tax liability. Yet even the Inland Revenue statistics‡ reveal that, in the financial year 1960–1, the number of people in the "millionaire group" of surtax payers with incomes of £100,000 a year and over increased from 63 to 81. Indeed, surtax payers in the large income groups had risen by 1590 in the space of 2 years, as the figures in Table 13 show.

A survey of personal incomes, before tax, for 1959–60 discloses that 81,340 people received £5000 or more a year.

* Cole, G. D. H., *The Condition of Post-War Britain.* His analysis was on the basis of 1954 figures.

† Titmuss, R. M., *Income Distribution and Social Change*, Allen & Unwin, London, 1961.

‡ Commissioners of Inland Revenue, *Report* for year ended 31 March, 1962; H.M.S.O., London, 1963.

TABLE 13

	Income (£s)	1959–60	1960–1
	15,000–20,000	3341	4119
	20,000–25,000	1372	1641
	25,000–30,000	632	878
	30,000–40,000	590	756
	40,000–50,000	226	300
	50,000–75,000	210	243
	75,000–100,000	58	82
Totals	15,000–100,000	6429	8019

A high income is, of course, one of the more obvious rewards of success in the commercial world. Although business men are still very secretive about themselves and their salaries,* more information is coming to light as the result of recent studies. The salaries of top executives probably range from, say, £8000 to £40,000, which is equivalent to a post-tax range of £3000 to £8000. This may seem proportionately lower than pre-war incomes, but it in no way reflects the business man's actual standard of living. He may enjoy a generous expense account plus benefits in kind from his firm; these "fringe" benefits could well double his net income. A survey of top management pay in seven countries†—including information supplied by 138 British companies—shows a positive correlation between the size of a firm and its top man's salary. At least in the middle ranges, if one firm is twenty times the size of another the odds are that it will pay its managing director twice as much. The head of an organization employing 1000 people typically earns £7000; the head of a firm of 20,000 employees would usually earn £14,000. The average British managing director's salary rose in 1960–1 by 7·7 per cent.

* Roy Lewis and Rosemary Stewart (*The Boss: The Life and Times of the British Business Man*, Phoenix, London, 1958) reveal that in a certain three-month period, the 203 obituaries in *The Times* included only twelve of business men compared with thirty-four of the armed forces.

† *Survey of Top Management Remuneration*, McKinsey & Co., Inc., U.S.A., 1962.

If the Marxist dichotomy were the sole criterion of class, there would be no problem at all—even Weber* argued that " 'property' and 'lack of property' are the basic categories of all class situations". Many of the middle classes, in this sense, would belong more appropriately to the proletariat, but propertylessness does not necessarily imply that unity of class interests which Marx hoped to find. Thus the propertyless classes differ widely as regards their "life chances"; so much so that Weber remarked "only persons who are completely unskilled, without property and dependent on employment without regular occupation, are in a strictly identical class position." Certainly the middle classes have never been strictly proletarian in terms of income, job security and occupational mobility. The higher incomes associated with non-manual jobs were originally a reward for scarcity, but are now retained as a status differential. In any case, in most industries clerical costs form only a small proportion of an employer's total costs. Relative immunity from the ups and downs of the trade cycle has always been the non-manual worker's prerogative. This may not be as important in a political climate when all major parties are committed to full employment, but it still carries an indefinable prestige value. Finally, the middle classes have a better chance of rising to managerial and supervisory posts, perhaps because of their closer relationship with those already in authority (in factories, clerical staff work in closer proximity to the management than do the manual employees), perhaps because of their superior educational qualifications, manners, etc.

Other factors important in any overall assessment of the middle classes include clothes and speech. At the turn of the century, the middle classes would undoubtedly have clearly declared their status by their clothing. Present-day affluence, improved techniques in the mass production and marketing of clothing and the influence of the mass media now mean that any attempt on the part of one section of the community to distinguish itself by its apparel can be quickly defeated if other people in the society also adopt the same fashion (viz., the upper-class innovation of Edwardian clothes with velvet

* Weber, M., *Essays in Sociology*, Routledge & Kegan Paul, London.

collars, immediately discarded when the lower class copied it*). There is no generalized middle-class "uniform", just as there is no universal middle-class accent. However, as Roy Lewis and Angus Maude† point out, if an ideal accent were not a necessary attribute of social status, Shaw would not have been able to write *Pygmalion*. One cannot ignore the influence of the B.B.C., too, in disseminating a sort of "accent-free" English.

Michael Young and Peter Willmott's study of Woodford,‡ a predominantly middle-class area in East London (the late Sir Winston Churchill was its M.P. until 1964), produced a report containing many significant observations, chiefly concerning the style of life of their informants.

> We saw something of the variety in people's lives as we went about our interviewing. Our informants sometimes engulfed us in deep, velvet-covered settees, and handed us glasses of sherry which we had to hold gingerly in the left hand while unchivalrously scribbling notes with the right. In another street we were seated on hard upright chairs next to drying nappies and given a large cup of the sweet tea and sterilized milk which we had come to know in Bethnal Green. . . . One [mother] would tell us she starts her day with grilled kidneys and coffee and ends it with "buttered cream crackers and cheese and port"; another that she begins with cornflakes and tea and ends with cocoa.

Throughout the area there was a constant preoccupation with material possessions: the £8000 house, the Rover 100, the extra-large refrigerator. This concern was not limited only to an attempt to raise one's own standard of living, but also depends on the desire to maintain status in the eyes of one's neighbours and the wider community. One husband told the interviewers that "As soon as next door knew we'd got a washing machine, they got one, too. Then a few months later we got a fridge, so they got a fridge as well." Another informant said that "During the course of conversation a

* See Fyvel, T. R., *The Insecure Offenders*, Chatto and Windus, London, 1961, for a valuable discussion on the significance of Edwardian fashions in the Teddy Boy period.

† Lewis, R., and Maude, A., *The English Middle Classes*, revised Penguin edition, 1953.

‡ Young, M., and Willmott, P., *Family and Class in a London Suburb*, Routledge & Kegan Paul, London, 1960.

neighbour told me they were getting a new car. Then she mentioned someone else in the road who's just got a new car, and she said, 'That'll be a knock in the eye for *them*'."

The corollary to the middle classes' desire to maintain their own separate identity was their equally strong determination to resist the encroachments of the working class. It was generally felt that higher wages did not necessarily make the workers *socially* higher than before. In fact, they were often looked down on more than ever. Two conventional stereotypes were frequently quoted: one that the British workman does not really work (this was supported by a company director, who remarked: "The working class is wrongly named because they don't work at all, judging by what happens in our firm"); the other that the working class do not know how to spend all their extra money. In this connection it is interesting to note that the working classes were not encouraged to spend their extra money at the local clubs, some of which controlled their membership lists by imposing exorbitant fees, while others used recommendation methods to maintain the exclusiveness of the organization.

The composition of the middle classes has changed enormously in the past 150 years: its upper levels have merged with the nobility, while the upper levels of the working class are now almost indistinguishable from the lower middle class. Clearly many individuals marginal to the middle class are experiencing the desire to identify themselves with the higher status group, and they seek to "bourgeoisify" themselves by limitations on family size, placing high value on education, and by emphasizing "respectability". It seems probable, therefore, that with so many individuals aspiring to middle class status, even those who easily qualify in terms of income alone, the position of the middle classes as a whole has never been so secure.

On the other hand, industrialization, the economics of mass production, and the social services have done much to eliminate the Marxian proletariat. Full employment has brought a narrowing of the wage differentials between skilled, semi-skilled and unskilled workers. Salary-earners have generally fallen behind in the incomes race since 1939, compared with wage earners. Consequently, the standard of living enjoyed by these various sections of the community has approached a common norm containing more elements of the old middle-class style than of the working-class manner. C. Wright Mills* describes the new middle classes as proletarian, by the Marxian definition of no longer owning the means of production, yet *bourgeois*, by virtue of their work situation, their evaluation of their own status, and their life chances in the new society. They are the technocrats and bureaucrats of the modern gigantic corporation. In the decline of the small businessman in contemporary America, Mills finds evidence to support the Marxist thesis that capital will become concentrated in fewer and fewer hands. However, the new middle classes still adhere to the ideology of the old middle classes, namely, that anyone can get to the top. These arguments have only a limited relevance to the British class situation, but their general importance is clear: that it is no longer practicable to define the middle classes merely in terms of income, or ownership of property. Today the middle classes rely on a status derived from their style of life, and to this extent the social changes in the working class have been a levelling up rather than a levelling down.

For this country, moreover, there is little basis for the suggestion that the new middle classes are exclusively founded on the "corporation man". Certainly the industrial and governmental bureaucracy represents an increasing proportion of the middle classes, but the 1951 census showed that there were still over 1½ million proprietors and managers of retail businesses, and shop assistants, while nearly one million people are engaged in agriculture. This is to say nothing of the professions (to be dealt with in a later section of this chapter) and women, many of whom would have thought it degrading to work at all in the nineteenth century, even at housework. Yet the position today is such that the working-class wife cannot be differentiated (on the criterion of her domestic duties) from her middle-class counterpart. Social gradings, if any, must be acquired in other ways, e.g. by the adoption of certain socially esteemed leisure pursuits. Here again the distinctions are becoming less significant with rising standards of living generally. Even if an individual cannot gain total social acceptance into a desired social class, he may at least take on the attributes

* Mills, C. W., *White Collar*, Oxford University Press, 1951.

of that class in one or more specific ways (its manners, its speech, its style of life) and this is half the battle towards full membership. Hoggart's vision* of "our emerging classlessness" is, I believe, in reality an individualistic interpretation of what he sees as the widespread adoption of values which are recognized as middle class and, *ergo*, desirable.

THE PROFESSIONS

In 1801, about 2 per cent of the employed population were professional people, while the corresponding figure for 1951 was 5 per cent. Today, between 1½ and 2 million men and women belong to the professions, whether salaried or fee-earning. This includes the qualified employees of banks and insurance companies, officers of the Armed Forces, and such nominally independent occupations as doctors, barristers, teachers, etc.

It is very difficulty to obtain a satisfactory definition of the characteristics of a professional occupation, especially since the qualities possessed by the older professions—such as the Church—differ from those held by the more recently created ones. This chapter will make no attempt to lay down whether particular occupations are true professions or not, but the problem of accurate nomenclature is typified by the various descriptions offered by Sir Alexander Carr-Saunders. In the 1928 Herbert Spencer Memorial Lecture he defined a profession as "an occupation based on specialized intellectual study and training, the purpose of which is to supply skilled service or advice for a definite fee or salary".

In conjunction with P. A. Wilson, Carr-Saunders wrote a book called *The Professions*,† published in 1933, in which the authors confessed themselves unable to improve upon the *Oxford English Dictionary*'s definition: "a vocation in which a professed knowledge of some department of learning or science is used in its application to the affairs of others or in the practice of an art founded upon it." Finally, in the *Report on Education for Commerce* (1947), Carr-

* Hoggart, R., *op. cit.*

† Carr-Saunders, A. M., and Wilson, P. A., *The Professions*, Oxford University Press, 1933.

Saunders again gave his verdict on a profession as: "any body of persons using a common technique who form an association, the purpose of which is to test competence in the technique by means of examination."

Reflected in these changing ideas is the changing position of many professional groups, part of a process that began, not in this century, but in the immediate aftermath of the Industrial Revolution. The origin of the professions lies in the increasing demands of trade in the Middle Ages, which created a demand for more and more master-craftsmen and professional men. Although these individuals have often been described as mere feudal retainers, it is now established that as early as the twelfth century they had become professional in the strict sense, giving their services in return for cash payments and salaries. However, the advent of capitalism and the Industrial Revolution provided the greatest impetus to the growth of the professions, since only the rise in living standards provoked by these events could bring respectability by such callings as medicine and education.

Various methods of classifying the professions may be employed, possibly into categories of occupations exhibiting certain common features. However, it is becoming increasingly difficult to distinguish the professions in terms of, say, their methods of remuneration, since members of the same vocation may be either fee-earning (an independent solicitor) or salaried (a solicitor employed by a private firm or a government department). This applies equally to medicine, architecture, engineering and journalism. Perhaps the most useful system of classification is that used by Lewis and Maude* when they group professions according to their relationships with the State in its widest sense, that is, the central government and local authorities. At one extreme are those professions where the State exercises a total monopoly of employment: the Civil Service, local government service, Armed Forces and the police. The second category includes all occupations in which public authorities provide employment for the majority of the profession's practitioners: teaching, nursing, medical auxiliaries. Thirdly, those vocations—

* Lewis, R., and Maude, A., *op. cit.*

such as medicine, dentistry, pharmacy—where the State provides considerable *part-time* employment; followed by those professions a substantial minority of which are employed by public authorities: architects, accountants, scientists, surveyors, librarians. Next comes a group where public authorities only employ a very small proportion of the profession's membership. but where the profession itself is subject to considerable State control or supervision: banking and stockbroking, the Church of England clergy. Finally, at the other extreme, are those professions whose members are comparatively free from State interference and who are scarcely employed by public authorities at all. This group includes a significantly small number of occupations, such as trade union officials, journalism, authors, actors, and possibly university teachers.

Although the validity of the above categories may be admitted, their usefulness is restricted except possibly to prove how few professions are not subject to direct or indirect control from the State—either as potential employers or as an explicitly regulatory body. Even those callings in the last group are liable to State control in certain circumstances. Thus journalism can be restricted indirectly by government limitations on the supply of newsprint, and the theatrical profession could be subjected to censorship stricter than that at present exercised. This question of externally imposed sanctions is vitally important because a profession cannot be recognized as such if it is subjected to excessive State interference. Yet it is recognized that, for example, if the Government insists on compulsory vaccination, or death certificates, it is entitled to specify the qualifications required by the doctor performing the vaccination or writing the certificate.

In general, a profession is characterized by three components: organization, training, and a code of conduct. Not all professions possess all three (e.g. actors), and not all occupations which do possess all three are recognized universally as professions (e.g. public relations officers), but for the purposes of this broad analysis we may ignore these rare exceptions.

In his 1947 definition of a profession, Sir Alexander Carr-Saunders specifically implied that a formal organization is the necessary corollary of a profession. He suggests that one of the functions of such an organization is to examine potential recruits "to test competence in the technique". However, this generalization is difficult to substantiate since some professional associations exist merely as learned societies (examples include the British Sociological Association and the Institute of Physics). Others exist primarily, if not solely, as middle-class equivalents of the trade unions, and indeed it is natural for the professions to be concerned about their economic rewards. This preoccupation occurs most frequently in those vocations whose members have direct contact with the public and charge fees for a personal service: the Law Society, in particular, lays down a fixed scale of fees for its members.

Training represents only one aspect of the methods employed by the professions to preserve their status and to justify their claims. Prior to the Industrial Revolution, entry into a profession was regulated in the same way as that into a craft, namely, by the control of apprenticeship. As the numbers of professions grew, and the intellectual ability required by each became greater, so the written examination became generally adopted, particularly after the adoption of the Northcote–Trevelyan reforms in the Civil Service. In addition, a few professions are "closed" in the sense that sanctions are practised against those who practise the calling and yet are excluded from the professional register. The British Medical Association, although not a "closed shop" in the legal sense, has enjoyed a combination of what Carr-Saunders and Wilson* call an "ingenious constitution admirably adapted to the needs of the case", and inspired leadership, to give doctors a greatly improved social status and professional standing. The State specifies that death certificates have to be signed by a registered medical practitioner, and this signature will be refused if a doctor has not been treating the individual. At the resulting inquest, a manslaughter charge may be preferred against any unregistered practitioner involved (such as a nature healer).

Just as the medical profession is theoretically open but in practice closed, so accountants need not, in principle, register as chartered accountants. If they do not, however, they lose the opportunity of

* Carr-Saunders, A. M., and Wilson, P. A., *op. cit.*

undertaking a good deal of lucrative work covered by, for example, the Friendly Societies Act. In fact, the Law provides one of the rare instances of a profession absolutely closed to all but registered practitioners, since unauthorized persons are prevented by statute from pleading in the courts. It would appear that the "closed shop" type of profession is restricted chiefly to the older vocations with a very definite fiduciary nature, where mutual trust between the person giving advice and the person seeking it is essential.

Most professional bodies have a code of conduct which is accepted by all their members, though the importance of this is much greater for those callings whose members characteristically offer independent advice and opinions in return for a fee. The public has to be assured that high fees are warranted by the absolute impartiality of the advice, and so certain professions are deeply concerned with the maintenance of the correct "public image" for their members. The acceptance of gifts, for example, is forbidden in the Royal Institute of British Architects' code of honour, since these might influence the advice given. If a particular profession were suspected of prejudice, then nobody would ask its advice, and its financial return would be nil.

The majority of the newer professions depend on their employers, to a greater or lesser degree, for the maintenance of an adequate code of ethics. If a salaried employee is asked to act in a way which he regards as unethical, he may appeal to his professional body for assistance. Thus, for example, in a dispute between workers and directors, a labour-relations manager (affiliated to the British Institute of Management) may find himself in the dilemma of either acting impartially or supporting one side in the quarrel. This, in fact, is a point against the proposition that managers do constitute a profession.

The great variety of specialized and expert occupations today reflects the growing specialization and division of labour which is a function of mature industrialization. Occupations become more skilled until the knowledge required for the performance of these occupations becomes sufficient to form the basis of a profession. Similarly, the increased dependence of production upon applied science means a tremendous growth in the number of scientific specialists. This new demand for vocational and professional training is not being met by the traditional forms of education. The universities, for example, generally confine themselves to training for the old-established professions (the Law and the Church) although at the present time there is growing support for the establishment of a post-graduate school of management studies attached to one of the universities and comparable with the Harvard Business School. Hence the training has to be supplied or supervised, or both, by new organizations which provide the basis for the specialisms' eventual claim to professional status. The signs are that this proliferation of the professions will continue, since it represents an upward movement as desirable, to those who make it, as the movement from working- to middle-class level. A few individual vocations are suffering a consolidation of their numbers. This category includes journalism, a victim of newspaper closures and amalgamations, and repertory acting, a victim of TV. Yet these cases are rare, and the majority of the evidence indicates that the professions still possess "incalculable strength and stability".*

* Lewis, R., and Maude, A., *op. cit.*

CHAPTER 4

Education

The right to a decent childhood is an absolute in a democratic and reasonably rich society. There is no conceivable justification for the intolerable start in life that we give so many. While chapel bells toll at Winchester, while wet bobs and dry bobs wander around the warmly red Tudor walls of Eton, while hundreds of pounds a year are spent on some children, there are hundreds of thousands to whom a good education is a three-decker school, erected at low cost, surrounded by asphalt, with no gymnasium, no laboratories, no playing fields, no pleasantness and adequacy at all.

(JOHN VAIZEY, "Facing Up to the School Bill," the *Observer*, 6th January 1963)

We rightly ask of our educational system that it should give equal opportunities to climb a ladder irrespective of income or social class.

(SIR EDWARD BOYLE (the then Minister of Education) in an interview with the *Guardian*, 6th September 1962)

One day I'll write a whole bloody treatise about how crummy education is in this smashing welfare state. I don't care how many mashers they string up for murder and arson, or how many tarts there are on the streets, or whether the state provides me with my pearly white dentures, but it makes me bloody boil to think of the rubbish most kids get taught before they're hoofed out at fifteen into the cold world.

(STANLEY PRICE, *Just for the Record*)

INTRODUCTION

The importance of education lies not only in its power as a factor in social stratification but also in the rather obvious fact that the prosperity of the country depends, ultimately, on the quality and quantity of education received by its citizens. A democracy can never work efficiently unless all its members possess at least a reasonable degree of literacy. It was the realization of this fact which led to the enforcement of elementary education for all in 1880, *after* the vote had been extended to almost all the male population. Similarly, an industrialized country can never maintain its prosperity, in the face of technological and economic competition, without continued attention to scientific training and the efficient deployment of manpower. Thus, for example, talent is wasted if a potentially gifted individual is forced to remain an agricultural labourer all his life, as often occurred before education became free and compulsory and competitive examinations replaced nepotism as the chief source of recruitment to most professions. This is an extreme example (as is that of Lord Morrison of Lambeth, who began life as an errand boy at the age of 12), but it can be applied throughout our society, whose increasing complexity creates a massive demand for the maximum utilization of potential skills *at every level*. This means an education system specifically designed to weed out, and make the most of, such aptitudes as may be possessed by the populace. This is not to say, however, that the argument for education is merely a question of economic utility. T. S. Eliot* points out that if education were designed solely to produce "equality of opportunity" (a view which Eliot calls "Jacobinism in education"), then this would not only be an unattainable ideal, but "if we made it our chief aim, [it] would disorganize society and debase education". It would disorganize society because it would replace classes by *élites* of intelligence (and the equal opportunity dogma is often quoted as a solution to class divisions), and it would debase education by restricting it to training for occupational success. Naturally, the latter is often uppermost in the minds of those who profit by their acquisition of educational qualifications, but most educational theorists, when asked the question: What is education *for*? would go further than the narrow economic justification. It is no part of this book to answer these philosophical inquiries, but it must surely be sufficient to add, almost in parentheses,

* Eliot, T. S., *Notes Towards a Definition of Culture*, Faber, London.

that our cultural heritage, the things that make us "civilized", are embodied in and can only be transmitted through education.

THE EDUCATIONAL SYSTEM

Table 14 illustrates the overall pattern of education provided by each of England's 146 local education authorities (L.E.A.s). It must be emphasized that this is little more than a very broad generalization, since each L.E.A. is virtually autonomous and is only subject to the administrative supervision of the Ministry of Education. Most of the theoretical writings on secondary education in England (e.g. the Hadow and Spens reports*) have emphasized a tripartite system, and the psychological force of this continual emphasis has been very powerful. Yet the freedom which L.E.A.s enjoy has led to the creation of a vast variety of secondary schools. Indeed, by 1958–9 the Ministry of Education had almost abandoned the statistical classification of secondary schools because they now include such an enormous range of types.

The local education authorities are made up of the English and Welsh administrative counties, the county boroughs (large towns or cities with powers similar to counties), and some "excepted districts". The latter (Swindon is an example) are areas within a county which have either an overall population of 60,000 or more, or a school population of over 7000. Any locality fulfilling these conditions may apply to become an "excepted district" by right, and others not quite satisfying the conditions may be granted the same privilege if the Minister of Education considers their claims to be justified. According to the 1944 Education Act, the duty of the Minister of Education is "to secure the effective execution by local authorities *under his control and direction* of the national policy for providing a varied and comprehensive educational service in every area" (my italics). The italicized phrases clearly indicate that, in the ultimate analysis, local education authorities are subordinate to the Ministry. Yet, as we have already seen, L.E.A.s are, in practice,

* The Hadow Report: *Education of the Adolescent*, H.M.S.O., 1926; the Spens Report: *Secondary Education with Special Reference to Grammar and Technical High Schools*, H.M.S.O., 1938.

subject to very few restrictions so long as their provision for education is "adequate".

TABLE 14

Age (years)	The State educational system (provided by) 146 L.E.A.s) — 95% of all children[1]			The private educational system (provided by preparatory and public schools) — 5% of all children
3	Nursery			
4	Nursery			
5	Infant			Private Junior
6	Infant			Private Junior
7	Junior			Private Junior
8	Junior			Preparatory
9	Junior			Preparatory
10	Junior			Preparatory
11	Secondary Modern	Others (Technical, Bilateral, etc.	Grammar	Preparatory
12	Secondary Modern	Others (Technical, Bilateral, etc.	Grammar	Preparatory
13	Secondary Modern	Others (Technical, Bilateral, etc.	Grammar	Preparatory / Public
14	Secondary Modern	Others (Technical, Bilateral, etc.	Grammar	Public
15	Secondary Modern	Others (Technical, Bilateral, etc.	Grammar	Public
16	. . . .	Others (Technical, Bilateral, etc.	Grammar	Public
17		. . . .	Grammar	. . . .
18		. . . .	. . . .	. . . .

[1] With the exception of the educationally subnormal, physically handicapped, etc., who *may* attend special schools.

Schooling is compulsory from the ages of 5 to 15. It may be begun earlier, at a nursery school or in the nursery department of a primary school, but this is comparatively rare, for the simple reason that most L.E.A.s place this aspect of education very low on their list of priorities. Indeed, some provide no nursery schools at all, while others only cater for a small proportion of the 3- to 5-year-old age group. At the other end of the stipulated 10 years, it is becoming increasingly common (and this perhaps reflects the growing popularity of education) for pupils in all types of school to remain there beyond the statutory leaving age, usually for some specific reason, such as the completion of a G.C.E. course.* Parents whose children attend grammar schools are almost invariably required to sign an undertaking to keep them at school until 16, since the grammar school's curriculum is based on G.C.E. and this is the age when Ordinary Level G.C.E. is normally taken. Although such agreements are not legally binding, they naturally exert great moral pressure, and the parent's willingness to sign may be a vital factor in the marginal child's chances of gaining admission to grammar school. Over a period of 8 years (1955–62), there has been a 72 per cent increase in the number of school-leavers with five or more Ordinary Level G.C.E. passes. For students with two or more Advanced Level passes, the increase has been more than 100 per cent. Part of the rise has been due to high post-war birth-rate and the variations in size of successive age-groups. But, even allowing for this, the figures show a 44 per cent and a 75 per cent increase in each category respectively.†

* It is depressingly necessary to note that in Dagenham, only 3·8 per cent of young people over the age of 15 are in full-time education, the lowest percentage among 150 towns surveyed in 1962. One probable reason for this was suggested by a headmaster: those who stay on "feel they are being isolated from their contemporaries". However, Dagenham is not a typical locality, and my generalization about the growing popularity of education still holds good. See Willmott, P., *The Evolution of a Community*, Routledge and Kegan Paul, London, 1963. Ministry of Education figures show that in January 1962 one-fifth of the 16-year-olds and one-tenth of the 17-year-olds who had received their education in maintained schools were still at school; in grammar schools, the proportion of 17-year-olds still at school rose from 30 to 44 per cent in 6 years. See *Statistics of Education*, Part I, H.M.S.O., 1963.

† 1962 *Statistics of Education*, Part III, H.M.S.O., 1963.

At the age of $10\frac{1}{2}$ a process of selection occurs, as a result of which about 25 per cent of children continue their education in grammar schools or in grammar "streams" in other schools. Approximately 66 per cent move to secondary modern schools; the rest are accepted by technical, comprehensive or bilateral schools.* The basis of the eleven-plus assessment is generally a combination of intelligence tests, attainment tests (particularly in arithmetic and English) proficiency tests in certain subjects, teachers' reports and primary school records. Local education authorities vary enormously in the importance they attach to each of these, and some may be omitted completely. Research has certainly indicated that the selection process can be faulty, so much so that Leicestershire now refuses to sort out its children at the age of 11, preferring to delay this until they have all had three years in a modern "high" school. According to the Leicestershire Plan, 14-year-old children may transfer to a grammar school if they wish. There is no selection examination, but the condition is laid down that those choosing this alternative must remain at school until 16. About 45 per cent are willing to accept these stipulations, and this represents most who are suitable for G.C.E. courses. Many of the remainder profit by a social studies syllabus at the modern school, involving visits to factories, careers lectures, etc. At the time of writing, the West Riding and Felixstowe are planning similar systems.

* In January 1962, the distribution of 13-year-olds at maintained secondary and all-age schools was as follows:

Type of school	%
Secondary Modern	64
Grammar	18
Comprehensive	5
Technical	3
Bilateral and multilateral	2
All-age	3
Other Secondary	5
Total	100

Source: Ministry of Education, *Statistics of Education*, Part I, H.M.S.O., 1963.

Although we have said that 25 per cent of all children at the secondary stage attend grammar school or the equivalent, this does not mean that the proportion is the same for all L.E.A.s. Indeed, it may vary between 40 per cent and 10 per cent, according to area and to the number of grammar school places provided. In other words, although the average Intelligence Quotient "cut-off" level for grammar school pupils might be 115, in some L.E.A.s it could rise to 125 or even higher while in others it could be as low as 105. Wallasey allows 32 children out of every 100 to go to grammar school, while in Burton on Trent only 13 do. Since the children are likely to have the same range of abilities, 19 children out of every 100 in Burton on Trent are being denied grammar school education which they would have had if they had lived in Wallasey. It is obvious that this discrepancy has important effects so far as equal opportunity is concerned.

Parents regard the grammar school as the home of an intellectual *élite* (even though the selection system is imperfect). The grammar school tends to concentrate on academic subjects, without any direct vocational application, rather than "technical" disciplines. This is not as true as it once was: science is playing an increasingly important part, and practical subjects, such as technical drawing, are creeping back into the curriculum. However, the syllabus is chiefly based on the General Certificates of Education (G.C.E.), administered by nine separate examining boards. Each is sponsored by the universities with the exception of the Associated Examining Board (set up in association with the City and Guilds Institute, to provide G.C.E. examinations with a slightly more technical bias). The fact that passes in G.C.E. subjects, at Ordinary and Advanced Levels, are essential for university entrance and for success in many white-collar professions, perhaps explains the anxiety of ambitious parents that their offspring should obtain access to grammar school.

If entry to grammar school is widely regarded as an "Open Sesame" to high occupational achievement, then, conversely, consignment to secondary modern school is widely regarded as an admission of failure, despite persistent assertions to the contrary by educationists. This mental chain-reaction stems from the immediate post-war period, when the declared ethos of modern schools comprised the somewhat negative doctrine that they would be free from the narrow, hide-bound teaching imposed by examination syllabuses. Instead, the teachers would be free to pursue any topic in which their pupils showed interest, without fear of wasting time more properly devoted to pre-examination work. The application of this belief meant that many children, of average intelligence, left the schools with no qualifications at all. Today, a significant majority train their more able pupils for G.C.E. while the less talented work for lower level examinations, such as those of the Royal Society of Arts, the Union of Educational Institutions, or the College of Preceptors. No doubt the introduction of a Ministry-sponsored Certificate of Secondary Education in the near future will do much to encourage this trend. To supplement these nationally recognized external examining bodies, modern schools in some areas have established their own locally administered qualifications, such as the Reading Certificate of Education. This fulfils two functions: it gives children an incentive to achieve a modest success in their 4-year period of secondary education. Furthermore, it helps employers select suitable applicants for their job vacancies. In some cases, unexpected success in these lower-level examinations may encourage pupils to remain at school and take G.C.E., producing, in effect, a *de facto* leaving age of 16 (which may become *de jure* if the recommendations of the 1944 Education Act and the Crowther Report are carried out).

Comprehensive and bilateral schools represent an attempt (not always successful) to obviate the problems caused by eleven-plus selection. Broadly speaking, a comprehensive school,* as its name implies, absorbs all children of secondary school age regardless of their intellectual ability. This, it is argued, overcomes the social stigma attached to the secondary modern school and its occupants. Once inside the comprehensive school, however, the children may be "streamed" as much as if they had gone to separate schools, though so far as the external essentials are concerned (such as uniform and facilities) they appear equal. Classes may be graded according to the pupils' overall ability, in which case the school becomes a conscious

* See Pedley, R., *The Comprehensive School*, Penguin Books, 1963.

amalgam of grammar, technical and modern stream. Alternatively, pupils may be placed in classes according to their ability in individual subjects. Thus, for example, a child may be in the A stream in art, but the D stream in mathematics and the C stream in English. This arrangement satisfies the proponents of the comprehensive theory in that each pupil usually excels in some sphere of his school endeavours, and subject streaming enables him to feel a strong sense of achievement in at least one course of study. A further advantage of comprehensive schools is their size, making it possible for specialist staff to be engaged for teaching, say, book-keeping and office arts. On the other hand, the large size of such schools may be a disadvantage if it forces the headmaster to concern himself almost exclusively with administrative details.

Bilateral schools, incorporating two streams of the traditional tripartite system, represent an uneasy compromise between strict tripartism and the comprehensive ideal. Some of the advantages of the comprehensive school are retained, such as the association between pupils of widely differing intellectual abilities which may encourage mutual understanding. But if, as is often the case, the bilateral school consists of little more than two separate establishments sharing the same campus, then it is difficult to see whether the juxtaposition is really worth while.

The third element in the Spens notion of the tripartite system is the technical school, which is supposedly of grammar level but devotes itself primarily to technical subjects like engineering and physics. However, the gap between it and the grammar school has narrowed very significantly in the last few years, partly as a result of the grammar school's increasing emphasis on scientific subjects, and partly because the technical schools themselves have been eager to avoid the charge of being too narrowly vocational. These pressures, towards more science in academic strongholds, and towards more liberal subjects in technical institutions, are bound to show themselves in a convergence between the two. The likelihood of convergence is further increased by the fact that the highest examination normally taken at technical schools—Ordinary National Certificate—is virtually the same standard as the G.C.E. Advanced level. (Higher

National Certificate is roughly equivalent to a pass degree and is normally studied on a part-time basis. Both H.N.C. and O.N.C. contain a pronounced practical emphasis as well as theoretical work, so that, in industry's eyes, possession of H.N.C. may be more valuable than a degree.)

As regards further education, Table 15 indicates the main sources of such advanced training in Great Britain, together with the numbers of students involved. Most of these institutions are colleges of further education in the widest sense, whatever fancy names they may possess, and this apparent variety is a consequent of the 1944 Education Act, which urged L.E.A.s to provide further education establishments to suit local requirements. Most of these colleges provide courses in various categories—technical, commercial, vocational, non-vocational, recreational.

TABLE 15

Full-time higher education in Great Britain, academic year 1961–2

Main types of institution	Number of students
25 universities[1]	118,400
10 colleges of advanced technology	10,300
7 national colleges or equivalent	1,000
Scotland	
15 central institutions (technical colleges)	4,500
7 colleges of education (teacher training colleges)	6,300
England and Wales	
25 regional (technical) colleges	9,900
300 other technical colleges and colleges of art	18,100
146 teacher training colleges	48,400
Approximate total of students (full-time or sandwich courses)	216,900

[1] This figure does not include the University of Sussex or any of the other new foundations.

In Great Britain the universities and the training colleges are the only institutions at the further education level which cater exclusively for full-time students. Of the 30,000 freshmen at present entering universities each year, by far the greater proportion are studying for a degree. In most cases this qualification is not directly related to the requirements of a particular profession (apart from law, medicine and education itself). Indeed, the universities have strenuously resisted any attempt to make them too narrowly vocational.

Each university is extremely jealous of its independence and of the maintenance of its academic standards. For this reason, a significant number of students fail their degrees or never remain at university long enough to take their final examinations; but even so, the pressure on university places is so great that it is estimated they will only be able to fill about half of the 500,000 places required in 1980.* With this problem in mind, a massive expansion of the existing universities is taking place, together with the creation of new foundations, at York, Colchester, Coventry, Canterbury, Lancaster and Norwich. Of course, a vital element in the universities' independence is their financial basis, and their most important source of money is the University Grants Committee, which dispenses funds allocated to it by H.M. Treasury. This does not mean, however, that the universities are under government control, but simply that they benefit from official patronage in much the same way as a provincial repertory theatre may benefit from Arts Council grants.

* In 1963 the first attempt was made to co-ordinate applications for university entrance in this country, and the Universities' Central Council on Admissions was set up, including all universities in England and Wales except Oxford and Cambridge. In its first report, the Council states that about 50,000 sixth-formers applied for the 27,000 places likely to be available in the autumn of 1963; as foreign students are at present excluded from this survey, the total number of applicants might well be 55,000. Until this scheme was introduced, it was impossible accurately to estimate the number of university applicants, because many sixth-formers applied to several universities at once. Although it is difficult to estimate how many potential students were automatically excluded because they failed to get the requisite two Advanced Level passes in G.C.E., even if half were refused admission for this reason this still left about 12,000 qualified students excluded through lack of places (the *Observer*, 17 February 1963).

Also outside the control of local education authorities are the Colleges of Advanced Technology, ten of which have been designated at the time of writing. These receive a direct grant from the Ministry of Education, though their status is such that they may soon be brought under the aegis of the University Grants Committee. Either way the C.A.T. has the advantage of freedom from L.E.A. control. Among the essential qualifications of a potential C.A.T. are the presence of an extremely well-qualified staff, who are expected to shed their low-level teaching and concentrate exclusively on a standard at least higher than O.N.C. Moreover, the National Council for Academic Awards (which confers the status of C.A.T.) insists that the courses provided must contain some liberal element, which may take the form of foreign languages (as at Northampton C.A.T.), management studies, etc. Another prerequisite of C.A.T. rank is the provision of an adequate and efficient library. Finally, the College must furnish reasonable residential facilities, since a C.A.T. is designed to meet a national, even an international need.

Membership of a professional organization, in the engineering and applied science fields, is normally obtained through a combination of examination success and practical experience. Though these organizations are very numerous and differ widely in the degree to which they gain social acceptance, they resemble each other in that they stipulate certificates and diplomas as more appropriate qualifications than a university degree, possibly because the former represent a less theoretical, academic approach. However, the National Certificate (obtained on a part-time basis) or the National Diploma (full-time) are not, in themselves, sufficient for professional status. The individual must also obtain "endorsements", i.e. passes in subjects (such as management studies) not directly related to his technical specialism. Furthermore, he must have been practising his profession for a given period of time. While O.N.C. and H.N.C. are still much sought after, O.N.D. and H.N.D. (the diploma qualifications) are declining in favour of the comparatively new Diploma in Technology (Dip. Tech.), which is the practical counterpart to the more academic university degree. For the most part,

Colleges of Advanced Technology are distinguished by their teaching at Dip. Tech. level *and* by their renunciation of elementary work.

Apart from the universities and the C.A.T.s, the third and final type of further education establishment which is outside the control of the local education authority is the National College. These were set up by the Government to meet certain highly specialized needs for technological training which an L.E.A. would be both unable and unwilling to provide. They concern themselves with such subjects as Aeronautics (Cranfield), Food Technology, Foundry Work, Rubber Technology, and Ventilating and Refrigerating. Like the C.A.T.s, these National Colleges receive a direct grant from the Ministry of Education.

Of the 250 technical colleges and colleges of art in Great Britain, the most important are the twenty-five specially designed regional colleges. These establishments, whose main source of finance is the local education authority, are also subject to influence by ten Regional Advisory Councils, although the latter have no clearly defined executive powers. Most of the work done in technical colleges as a whole is directly related to particular occupational requirements, although this does not apply to evening classes, where only about a third of the courses are vocational (nearly a half are recreational, and the rest devoted to general education).

Industrial training may be subdivided into three main grades. The highest is that of *technologist*, who may have a university degree plus practical experience, or who could have attended a sandwich course in a C.A.T. or one of the larger technical colleges. Alternatively, he may have reached technological status through the part-time route, involving H.N.C., "endorsements", and a professional qualification. With regard to sandwich courses, these usually consist of alternate periods in college and in industry. If the student is college-based, then the college arranges with different firms to provide him with practical experience. More commonly, students are recruited by a company, paid a trainee's salary, and handed over to the college for theoretical tuition. The advantage of the former arrangement is that the college can organize the course on wider lines, with more emphasis on liberal studies. On the other hand, the company-based trainee is paid a good salary and the college does not have to worry about his future occupational placement. Sandwich courses vary from that provided by Ford (one week in college, followed by two weeks in industry) to that sponsored by Rolls-Royce, involving one year in the firm, three years at university for an engineering degree, followed by another year with the firm. In the latter scheme, the student also works for Rolls-Royce in the university vacations.

At the *technician* level, the educational requirement may be O.N.C. or H.N.C.: exactly where the individual reaches his maximum attainment will depend on his own abilities. The source of the technician's training may be much the same as that of the skilled *craftsman*, involving part-time day release, evening classes (with the company providing some motivation for continued attendance usually in the form of a monetary reward), or day release. In the case of craftsmen these courses lead towards Intermediate or Final City and Guilds Certificates plus, in certain industries (such as printing), a further certificate at full technological level. Far too common still is the type of craftsman's training which comprises no theoretical tuition at all and only a very limited form of practical training, known colloquially as the *Watch Old Joe* technique. Day release usually means one day a week at the local technical college; very few firms allow two days, and the number is decreasing. This type of instruction is chiefly provided for industrial and commercial apprentices, craftsmen and draughtsmen. In addition, some companies give day release for non-vocational studies (these include Cadbury, Marks & Spencer, the Metal Box Company and the G.P.O.).

The picture that emerges of our further education is predominantly a part-time structure. The technical colleges contain nearly 500,000 part-time students plus two million pupils at evening classes. Indeed, the proportion of part-time tuition seems even greater when it is recalled that nearly half of the colleges' *full-time* students are under 18 years old, and are therefore undertaking courses more appropriate to secondary schools. Although students attending full-time day courses have multiplied sixfold between 1931 and 1955, and evening enrolments have rather less than doubled, the biggest increase, fifteenfold, has been in the realm of part-time day release.

That this emphasis has not been advantageous is pointed out by the Crowther Report,* which argues that the wastage involved in part-time education is far too high. With evening classes, of course, the great majority of students never complete the courses for which they enrol. There are some signs that this fact is beginning to be appreciated by the authorities responsible for further education, particularly as the need increases for properly trained and qualified personnel at all levels in industry, but at present the difficulty lies in creating enough full-time places in technical colleges for those who require them.

The Robbins Report,† published in October 1963, has made radical proposals for the expansion of higher education. Compared with 216,000 places in full-time higher education available in 1962–3, the Report prophesies a need for 560,000 places in 1980–1. The statistical work behind this recommendation fills Appendix I of the Report and demolishes the "more means worse" or "pool of ability" school of arguments. Of the 560,000 places, 350,000 should be in the universities, i.e. the existing universities, six new foundations, translated C.A.T.s and promotions among the regional colleges, Scottish central institutions and training colleges. In addition, the Report recommends the creation of five "SISTERS" (Special Institutions for Scientific and Technological Education and Research), of which the first, Imperial College, London, has already been designated. Despite its controversial advocacy of a separate Ministry for Higher Education, the Robbins Report is widely seen as the forerunner of a radical programme of reform and expansion in higher education.

Technical colleges play some part in the provision of adult classes in this country, and the 1944 Education Act spoke of an obligation on L.E.A.s to "secure the provision for their area of adequate facilities for further education." However, the 1954 Ashby Report on adult education‡ showed that "by far the greatest burden of liberal adult

* The Crowther Report: *15 to 18*, Vol. I of the Report of the Central Advisory Council for Education (England), H.M.S.O., 1959. Vol. II (*Surveys*), H.M.S.O., 1960.

† Committee on Higher Education, Report, H.M.S.O., 1963.

‡ *The Organization and Finance of Adult Education in England and Wales*, H.M.S.O., 1954.

education is shouldered by responsible bodies and not by L.E.A.s". In England and Wales there are forty-three "responsible bodies", chiefly including the university extra-mural departments, and the Workers' Educational Association.

Most universities maintain extra-mural departments to provide adult classes lasting, generally, for a full academic year. Indeed, these 1-year courses are usually designed to lead directly to subsequent 3-year tutorial classes. If the universities supply short courses, many of these are intended for people who already have some experience of the subject, in which case the class is really comparable with high quality refresher tuition. Even a 6-week (i.e. six-lecture) course undertaken by the universities will not necessarily be of a lower standard than a longer course. The catchment areas for the extra-mural boards are not confined to the immediate environs of the university itself but, as in the case of Oxford (which also has centres in North Staffordshire, Lincoln and Kent), may extend over a considerable and apparently illogical area. However, the development of these provinces does not prevent close co-operation between the universities and with the other organizations responsible for adult education. For example, the W.E.A. is almost invariably represented on the extra-mural boards.

In 1954–5, there were nearly a thousand W.E.A. branches in the country, and total branch and district membership was approximately 35,000. The W.E.A. districts correspond roughly with the extra-mural areas, and the W.E.A. as a whole sets great store by its partnership with the universities. On the other hand, the W.E.A. may act independently in providing adult classes, and in localities where mutual consultation and co-operation are not as effective as they might be, there is considerable danger of overlapping with the extra-mural boards. As distinct from the 1-year courses arranged by the universities, those held by the W.E.A. are usually self-contained. In general W.E.A. courses are less exacting: this applies particularly to the classes of shorter duration. A typical W.E.A. programme concentrates on liberal studies, such as appreciation of the Arts and Literature, Social Science, History, Psychology, International Affairs, Geography, Philosophy and Religion. Class fees comprise only a small part of the W.E.A.s income—the majority is derived from the Ministry of Education (a grant to help pay teaching costs), grants and contributions from trade unions and industry, etc.

Both the universities and the W.E.A. collaborate, to varying degrees, with the local education authorities. The latter, on the whole, are content to secure the provision of adult education facilities rather than to provide such classes themselves (the exceptions to this rule include Kent, Glamorgan and London). Where L.E.A.s provide evening institutes, their courses primarily concentrate on vocational or recreational topics, such as foreign languages for those who intend to holiday abroad, choral singing, economics and history. In general, however, the L.E.A.s contribution to adult education is chiefly in the realm of financial aid—grants to universities and other "responsible bodies" to supplement the Ministry allowance—and the provision of free accommodation for adult classes in L.E.A. schools.

This century has truly seen the evolution of the secondary grammar school as the chief source of recruitment to the universities and the professions. Some of these schools had a long and honourable history; others had been established by local education authorities under the 1902 Balfour Act. Whatever their origin, they were characterized by their emphasis on academic subjects as distinct from practical disciplines. Today, there are around 1300 maintained grammar schools in England and Wales, of which about a third are for boys, a third for girls and a third co-educational. The average school has just over 550 pupils and most have between 300 and 800; only about 110 grammar schools provide any boarding places. In 1900, admission to such schools depended either on parental wealth or on exceptional promise shown in the elementary stage. In 1963, grammar school education depends more than anything else on the child's I.Q. and his chronological position within a specified age-range. Moreover, secondary education as a whole is now an accepted phase in the whole educative process, whereas in 1900, for most children, teaching stopped at elementary school. Credit for the change may be partly attributed to the 1926 report of the Hadow Commission* on the problem of post-primary education, which

* The Hadow Report, *op. cit.*

recommended that at the age of 11 *all* children should proceed to some form of secondary education. Three types of school were recommended to meet the estimated demand: secondary grammar, junior technical, and "modern" schools. Broadly speaking, these schools could be differentiated in terms of the educational attainment of their pupils, although the Hadow Commission preferred to confine themselves to the remark that the "modern" schools would have a more practical and vocational bias. Theoretically, the new "modern" schools (in some cases no more than senior departments to existing elementary schools) were to enjoy "parity of esteem". In practice the staffing ratio and equipment was almost invariably less generous than in the grammar schools. Of the technical schools, some of which had existed since 1900, the 1938 Spens Report had more to say, namely, that they should enjoy equality of status with the grammar schools but that after the age of 13 the pupils would specialize in more practical subjects.

The idea of the tripartite system, first mooted in 1868, was further reinforced by the 1943 Norwood Report.* Norwood reiterated the assumptions made by Hadow and Spens, that at the age of 11 all children should pass into secondary schools, of which there should be three types (grammar, technical, and "modern"). All three should enjoy parity of conditions and amenities. There should be a broadly common curriculum for the first 2 years at all schools, to facilitate transfer for late developers. Pressure from the Norwood Committee and the cumulative effects of earlier Commissions led directly to the 1944 Education Act, which revolutionized secondary education and incorporated the then novel concept of equality of opportunity. Henceforth no child, however poor his parents, would be denied access to the type of secondary education most suited to his intelligence and aptitudes. The adoption of this principle, and its obvious implications for the universities and the public schools, was to preoccupy politicians and sociologists for some years to come.

Nowhere does the Act mention the typical tripartite arrangement

* The Norwood Report: *Curriculum and Examinations in Secondary Schools*, H.M.S.O., 1943.

of grammar, technical, and "modern" schools, since this would have been regarded as unnecessarily restrictive so far as the future progress of education was concerned. Indeed, local education authorities are free to pursue any plans they wish and, as we have already seen, there exists enormous variety of provision for post-primary tuition. The school-leaving age was raised to 15 in 1947. It will probably become 16 as soon as availability of accommodation and other factors make this a practical proposition; recommendations along these lines were embodied in the Crowther and Newsom reports. Already a tentative step in this direction has been taken inasmuch as from September 1963 onwards there have been only two school-leaving dates per year, Easter and July. The importance of this development lies in the fact that it provides improved scope for coherent courses in the final year at school.

Clearly the enforcement of school attendance until 15, coupled with the 1944 Act's demand that secondary schools should be housed in different buildings from primary schools, created great pressure on education authorities, in terms of both financial resources and teacher recruitment. This pressure, at its height during the onset of the post-war austerity, has prevented the improvement in educational facilities from keeping up with the rise in the school population (to nearly 7 million).* However, the Ministry's insistence on certain building standards, the drive to abolish the all-age village schools, the striving towards a maximum of thirty pupils per class, the increased spending on new buildings—all these factors have, in recent years, helped to fill the gap. Between 1947 and 1959, nearly 2000 new secondary schools were built, compared with over 3000 primary schools. Many children in "modern" schools are remaining there longer than they need. There has been a remarkable increase in the numbers of G.C.E. candidates, both at Ordinary and at Advanced Level. Finally, considerable attention is being paid to expansion of

* An increase of nearly 2½ million is expected by 1985, of which half will be in the 5–10 age group. In fact, this is probably a conservative estimate, since the latest information from the Government Actuary suggests that the birth rate in the late 1960's will be between 50,000 and 60,000 higher than had been assumed.

the teacher training colleges and to the recruitment of teachers from the universities.*

In 1939, as a result of private enterprise and State action, there existed a wide variety of organizations providing further education. Those organizations included technical colleges, evening institutes, the Workers' Educational Association, university extra-mural departments, Women's Institutes, youth organizations (Y.M.C.A., Boy Scouts, community centres, etc.), and public libraries. It is impossible to say with any certainty just how many people benefited from these facilities, but in all (and including the universities) probably about 2 to 3 million were involved.

Until 1944, legislation was permissive rather than compulsory. Section 41 of the 1944 Education Act states that local education authorities *must* provide or secure the provision of a youth service, adult education for older people, and vocational training in technical, commercial and art colleges. As a result, the Ministry of Education figures for 1959 showed a 56 per cent increase in the number of students at major further education establishments and evening institutes since 1937. More particularly, there had been a great expansion in the number of workers given day release for education and training (from 42,000 in 1937 to 438,000 in 1959). Even this increase, as Venables† points out, only represents about one-third of the *potential* number of day-release students. In 1960 there was a slight decline in the figures—down to 406,000—but this may be attributable to the increasing tendency for pupils to remain at school beyond the statutory period, or the more generous facilities for full-time further education. Indeed, between 1937 and 1958 the numbers of full-time further education students rose from 20,000 to 124,000. Another significant trend has been the vast improvement in the quality of work at the technical colleges—so much so that many now provide courses of degree status or opportunities for post-graduate research.

* The Robbins Report, concerned with both, has suggested that training colleges should be renamed ("colleges of education") and should increase their places by over 75 per cent between 1970 and 1980.

† Venables, P. F. R., *Technical Education: Its Aims, Organization and Future Development*, Bell, London, 1955.

In the immediate post-war period, the Ministry of Education was naturally preoccupied with building primary and secondary schools. Its figures show that, between 1946 and 1952, over twenty-seven times as much money was spent on primary education as on further education. More recently, however, the Government, conscious of the vital connection between technology and economic survival, has been treating further education with increasing urgency. A number of reports* had repeatedly advocated the development of advanced courses of technology within technical colleges, the creation of new technological awards of degree status, and increased Exchequer aid. As the second half of the century opened, these pleas began to be heard. The Government is now committed to a massive expansion of the universities, particularly science departments.

Furthermore, in July 1955 the Minister of Education announced the establishment of the National Council for Technological Awards. Having created the Dip. Tech., the Council subsequently originated a higher award, comparable with the university distinction of Ph.D., and to be known as Membership of the College of Technologists. Courses leading to the Dip. Tech. and research leading to M.C.T. are chiefly provided by the C.A.T.s, although some technical colleges are recognized for Dip. Tech. tuition in particular subjects, e.g. Hatfield for aeronautics. Simultaneously with these developments in technological education, rapid progress was being made in increasing the facilities for training technicians and craftsmen, and the 1961 White Paper *Better Opportunities in Technical Education*† specifically advocated the extension of these lower-level courses.

SOCIAL ASPECTS OF THE EDUCATION SYSTEM

We have already seen that, for the most part, education in the eighteenth and nineteenth centuries was either inadequate or non-

* Special Committee on Higher Technological Education: Report (Chairman, Lord Eustace Percy), 1944; National Advisory Council on Education for Industry and Commerce: Report, 1950.

† *Better Opportunities in Technical Education*, Command 1254, H.M.S.O., 1961.

existent for the majority of the population. Access to satisfactory tuition was limited virtually to those whose economic position made this possible. This close correlation between the type of education received and one's socio-economic status has persisted throughout the history of education as embodied in the public schools (which will be analysed more closely in the next section of this chapter). Even when the 1868 Schools Inquiry Commission recommended the establishment of three types of secondary school, these were to be distinguished by social gradings rather than by the mental abilities of the pupils. Thus children of well-to-do parents would be taught the classics and similar non-vocational subjects up to the age of 18; children from the middle strata of society would receive an education suited to their eventual position as artisans, up to the age of 16; and the rest would receive, up to 14 years of age, an education to fit them to be labourers. This scheme was based on the widely accepted assumption that an individual's occupation should depend primarily, if not completely, on his social origins and that the lower classes should not be educated above their station in life. In other words, carried to its extreme the result would be a caste system of the worst kind. Fortunately, in 1870 the Civil Service Commission had replaced nepotism by competitive examination as its chief method of recruitment. This decision was to have far-reaching repercussions on education as a whole.

Pressure towards the large-scale provision of secondary education mounted during the early years of this century. Yet, of boys born between 1910 and 1929, only 14 per cent of those from State elementary schools were able to proceed to secondary school. This pressure originated from educationists, from Socialists like R. H. Tawney,* and from the frustrated pupils themselves. During this period, too, intelligence testing became far more sophisticated, and changing ideas about intelligence demolished the aristocratic ideal based on the Platonic notion of the division of humanity into superior and inferior classes.

The 1944 Education Act finally submitted to these pressures and attempted to remedy the situation. Henceforth, all children were to

* Tawney, R. H., *Secondary Education for All*, London, 1924.

receive the type of secondary education most appropriate to their abilities and aptitudes, and social origins were to be irrelevant. Yet the class implications of the educational system have never been more bitterly debated than they are now, and the blame for this has generally been placed at the door of tripartism. H. C. Dent* argues that the grammar school has always concentrated upon the acquisition of superior social status. Banks† clearly sees the grammar school as an agent of social selection. This fact, whose origin lies in the curriculum of the nineteenth-century endowed schools as the training ground of the *élite* blackcoated occupations, does much to explain the struggle for grammar school places at the present time. Furthermore, it explains why the driving force in education has been the desire for social status rather than the desire for education as such. The "literary" emphasis in the grammar school's curriculum, too, could be attributed to the fact that this type of tuition was thought to be more suitable for budding teachers and clerks. Certainly, a "literary" education is not an essential part of the equipment of those whose career expectations are oriented towards commerce, but it may be that such an education was originally encouraged because it seemed more "gentlemanly" than science. Even today a white-collar occupation is accorded high prestige, despite the assiduous publicity and financial incentives devoted since 1945 to the advancement of science. As Banks remarks, it is still true that the status of the grammar schools is borrowed from the occupations for which their pupils are being prepared. This being so, parity of esteem among all types of secondary education is nothing but an idle dream. It is worth noting that esteem has nothing to do with school buildings and equipment, as the secondary modern schools are often supplied with up-to-date materials in recently erected premises.

In short, then, more and more parents are realizing a truth which has been self-evident since the adoption of competitive examinations as the chief source of entry into the major professions, namely, that

* Dent, H. C., *The Educational System of England and Wales*, University of London, 1961; see also, *Secondary Education for All: Origins and Developments in England*, Routledge & Kegan Paul, London, 1949.

† Banks, J. A., *Parity and Prestige.*

education can be the passport to the relative security and prestige associated with white-collar occupations. The significance of this trend becomes even more overwhelming when one recalls the vast expansion (due to the increasing complexity of production, marketing, accounting, management, etc.) of professional and semi-professional occupations, all requiring educational qualifications of some kind. These occupations cover a large range of desirable positions, especially in the middle areas of the job hierarchy. As automation proceeds and mental skills replace manual skills, so the opportunities for entering professional occupations will increase. Conversely, the degree of ostracism attached to occupations of a lower status may tend to perpetuate a division in society between "success" and "failure", between grammar school and, for want of a better word, non-grammar education. Because the grammar schools are recognized as an essential preliminary to entry into a coveted range of professions therefore, the crucial role of such schools is as a determinant of future occupation.

A separate problem concerns class representation in the schools themselves; that is, having admitted that grammar schools provide a superior education in every sense of the word, do all social classes have an equal chance of obtaining such education? Certainly the intention of the 1944 Education Act was to throw open entry to the grammar schools to everyone on equal terms, regardless of social origin. Yet a multitude of studies have revealed that the middle class is heavily over-represented and the lower working class (with about 15 per cent of grammar school places) is proportionately under-represented. To express this another way, children from professional and managerial families account for 15 per cent of the total population, 25 per cent of the grammar school population, and 44 per cent of the sixth-form population. The H.M.S.O. report *Early Leaving* makes the point that there is a steady decline in academic performance from children as one progresses down the social scale. Thus, even if a working-class child is admitted to grammar school, his performance there is likely to be below average, he will probably leave before the sixth form, and he rarely reaches university.

A mass of new statistical evidence, collected by the National

Survey of Health and Development of Children since 1946, supports these comments. Covering a sample of more than 5000 British schoolchildren, the survey suggests that a third of the primary school pupils who should have gone to grammar school, judged by their ability at 8, did not in fact get there. Taking their ability at the time of the eleven-plus selection examination, a quarter of the children who should have got places were excluded—and virtually all these children came from poorer-than-average family backgrounds. When the eleven-plus results of the children who showed slightly above-average ability (I.Q. 105) at the age of 8 were compared, it was revealed that only 12 per cent of the children of lower manual working-class parents subsequently went to grammar schools, compared with 46 per cent of upper middle-class children. The lower manual working-class children, whose intelligence (as measured by I.Q. tests) seemed to fall by an average of several points between 8 and 11 years old, were further penalized by the working of the selection examination itself. For those at the margin (with I.Q.s of between 100 and 110), especially in areas where there were relatively few places in grammar schools, the examiners may have been unconsciously prejudiced in favour of a neat and clean appearance as distinct from a good academic record. Parental attitudes to work were of crucial importance: most children in the lower manual working class already had lower than average ability at 8, and this was observed to decline quite sharply if their parents took little interest. Another important factor revealed by the same survey was the standard of housing, inasmuch as unsatisfactory home conditions did not affect upper middle-class children very much between the ages of 8 and 11, but caused the children of lower manual working-class parents to drop about half a point in I.Q.

What are the causes of this phenomenon? Genetic factors may be a contributory element, but one would normally expect the large number of working-class children to counteract the high proportion of intelligent children in the middle class. This begs the question slightly, inasmuch as it admits the possibility that most middle-class children are of above-average intelligence. This may well be true if we also assume that middle-class membership is chiefly based on occupations which demand the application of considerable intellectual ability, and that parents normally have children whose intelligence closely approaches their own. However, heredity can only be a partial, not a sufficient explanation; a full analysis must take account of such social factors as the size of the family, parental contributions to the child's development, crowded and noisy homes, financial difficulties, etc.

Floud, Halsey and Martin* show that the size of the family is the dominant factor in environmental influence on educational chances. There can be no doubt that children from small families, whatever their social origin, tend to do better in intelligence tests and therefore in the grammar-school selection procedure. Needless to say, working-class families are likely to have more children than those in the upper levels of society. Several reasons have been suggested for apparent backwardness of children in large families. Dr. Nisbet, for example, suggests that the latter type of child learns verbal skills less effectively from his contemporaries than does the only child, who has far greater opportunities for conversing with adults. Evidence from Middlesbrough suggests that the disadvantages of a large family are less marked for Catholics, probably because intelligent Catholics do not practise family limitation. Thus the general level of intelligence among large Catholic families is higher than that among large non-Catholic families (where birth control is largely a function of intelligence).

An important problem for the working-class child concerns the parental attitude to education and its value. Brian Jackson's and Dennis Marsden's *Education and the Working Class* is a close study of eighty-eight clever working-class children in a northern town who made their way into the middle class by means of the grammar school. The children soon found it desirable to adapt their broad Yorkshire accents into standard English at school; yet if they spoke standard English at home they were regarded with contempt. Some attempted to meet their parents half-way: one got a holiday job on the railway, and remarked: "I enjoyed working with my hands. I felt

* Floud, J., Halsey, A. H., and Martin, F. M., *Social Class and Educational Opportunity*, Heinemann, London, 1956.

quite proud and when I came home at night, since I was not half as tired as I thought I would be, I used to say to my parents: 'There you are, you see!' because it's funny: my parents have a queer idea of work. Reading a book is not work; only doing things with your hands." Other children made no attempt to bridge the gap, and one of the subjects said: "I thought my parents were terrible, and very badly educated. They were always doing the wrong things." On the other hand, of course, the Jackson–Marsden study refers to the situation as it was some years ago, and more recently it is evident that a social revolution has taken place in parents' attitudes towards their children's education, particularly in the lower reaches of the social scale. Floud, Halsey and Martin* reported that in both Middlesbrough and south-west Hertfordshire, "numerous" working-class parents expressed a willingness to keep their children at grammar school until 16 years old. One-quarter of the Middlesbrough group even contemplated a leaving age of 18. Conversely, very few parents ever refuse a grammar school place for their child; although this may be mainly due to the increasing value placed on education, it must also be attributed, in part, to the reduced incidence of material factors. Poverty caused ill-health and low attendance at school; study facilities were absent in the slums; families would desperately need the extra income provided by adolescent earnings. None of these considerations is relevant today. Indeed, parents in difficulty may obtain extra financial assistance for their children's education.

One possible reason for the comparative under-representation of the working class in the grammar schools may derive from an unsympathetic interpretation of the phrase "capacity to profit". The "grammar marginals"—those children who in Intelligence Quotient terms are on the borderline of acceptance into grammar schools—are more likely to be given the benefit of the doubt if they are of middle-class origin. This is because teachers know grammar schools to be, by and large, middle-class centres with a middle-class ethos and therefore foreign to the working-class child. Furthermore, because middle-class parents generally have a high level of aspiration,

* Floud, J., Halsey, A. H., and Martin, F. M., *op. cit.*

their offspring are less likely to be premature school-leavers. The question of assimilation, according to *Social Class and Educational Opportunity*, is a vital problem to a child whose whole domestic environment clashes with the atmosphere of the grammar school. The authors suggest that the comprehensive school is a tentative solution, though this may be unsatisfactory in other respects.

If all these matters seem of trivial importance and unlikely to affect the overall picture of educational opportunity, then the conclusions of the 1959 Crowther Report* will soon put the situation into its correct perspective. The report advocates raising the school-leaving age to 16, and the introduction of compulsory part-time education from 15 to 18. One of the main arguments put forward to substantiate this recommendation is the tremendous wastage of talent in this country. In the mid-1950's two-fifths of the top 10 per cent of able boys left school at 16 and two-thirds of the next 20 per cent left at 15. Among girls the situation is worse. There is no doubt that if all working-class children of high academic ability went on to the universities there would be either many more students than at present, or the existing numbers would include a much higher proportion of working-class students. The report considered that most families can now support their children during a longer education, what with earlier marriages, fewer children, employment for wives, and the general increase in the standard of living.

Clearly much remains to be done before the expressed intention of the 1943 White Paper on *Educational Reconstruction*†—to provide equality of educational opportunity—can be satisfactorily fulfilled. Before this can happen, education must eradicate the notion that children can be divided into three types, each requiring a different system of secondary school and, to some extent, a different leaving age. As C. A. R. Crosland‡ and D. V. Glass§ point out, complete equality of educational opportunity can never be attained so long as the independent public school system is left to provide tuition for

* Crowther Report, *op. cit.*

† *Educational Reconstruction*, H.M.S.O., 1943.

‡ Crosland, C. A. R., *The Future of Socialism*, Cape, London, 1956.

§ Glass, D. V. (ed.), *Social Mobility in Britain*, Routledge & Kegan Paul, London, 1954.

children whose chief claim for admission to such schools is the possession of wealthy parents.

THE PUBLIC SCHOOLS

The public schools are usually taken to mean the better-known boarding schools, of which there are about eighty. A more precise definition may be derived from the Headmasters' Conference, whose membership is restricted to a maximum of 200, including girls' schools. The most vital qualification for admission to this select body (at present there are about 190 schools represented) is "the measure of independence enjoyed by the governing body and the headmaster". In other words, although some direct-grant grammar schools (supervised by the Ministry of Education, but free of local control) may be eligible, schools maintained by the local education authority are not. Other organizations associated with the private school system include the Independent Schools Association Incorporated, membership of which is limited to "the Heads of schools which are not under the direct control of the Ministry of Education and do not receive grants from the State", and also the Incorporated Association of Preparatory Schools.

Originally, the public schools were founded to provide a source of recruitment to the Church and the Law: Winchester, for instance, was formed to supply students to New College, Oxford. Until the end of the eighteenth century the schools largely catered for children in their respective localities, and many comparatively poor individuals achieved positions of eminence through them; in other words, they were definitely a channel of upward mobility. But, as the ex-pupils achieved prestige, this was reflected on to the *alma mater* and the schools began to lose their local character. During the nineteenth century about seven of the schools had gained a reputation as national boarding schools and their pupils were primarily fee-payers. It was at this time that the aristocracy began to patronize the public schools (which, of course, increased their prestige still further) instead of employing private tutors. Some headmasters remained conscious of their obligations towards the poor, despite opposition from fee-paying pupils' parents. Various devices were adopted, such as segregation in the playgrounds, but headmasters eventually succumbed and the public schools assumed the character which they have maintained, virtually unchanged to this day. Although local education authorities since 1944 have been able to take advantage of a small proportion of the vacancies arising at the public schools, the majority of the pupils are fee-paying. In all, the member schools of the Headmasters' Conference account for about 5 per cent of children in the 13-year-old age group.

We are not here concerned directly with the type of education offered by the public schools, although the predominantly classical curriculum offered in the nineteenth century has been watered down considerably by increased concentration on science teaching. More relevant, in this context, is the extent to which the public schools inhibit the complete attainment of equality in educational opportunity. There is little doubt that a public school training conveys a unique advantage on those fortunate enough to have experienced it. In some obvious respects, the best public schools are superior to the majority of those in the State system. For example, the staffing ratio is higher (at Eton, one teacher to every 11·5 pupils, compared with 1 : 21 in State schools in 1959).* The academic quality of the staff is better, and more satisfactory extra-curricular activities are provided. As C. A. R. Crosland† points out, even if these advantages were confined to the thirty or so major public schools, the others would still be able to confer a *social* superiority foreign to the State schools. Perhaps because of the boarding element, the public school product is widely believed to be more dependable and self-reliant and to possess a "better" accent, bearing and manners than his local authority educated counterpart. Norwood‡ remarks, for example, that an individual's social background is often judged by his pronunciation of "strange change" or "round the town".

* The ratio in grammar schools is 1 : 18, but the "weighted" ratio, allowing for differences in size of sixth forms, is much more nearly equal to that of the best public schools. In the State schools, a further 60,000 teachers is needed to get rid of oversize classes, according to *Staffing the Schools* (Ministry of Education, 1963).

† Crosland, C. A. R., *op. cit.*

‡ *The English Tradition of Education.*

Christopher Hollis* admits that one of the main motives behind sending children to Eton is the desire to give them a social headstart in life (an interesting additional motive concerns the social prestige acquired by *parents* who have a son at Eton).

In the past, the public schools have relied largely upon the existence of a permanent nucleus of wealthy couples who have been prepared to pay for their children's education over a period of some 6 years at least. Today, however, the significance of wealth, and particularly inherited wealth, has been very much reduced by the deliberate operation of income tax, surtax, death duties, etc., so that both the size and quantity of personal fortunes have declined. Yet the demand for public school places is, if anything, greater than ever. How has this happened? Certainly the reasons include the belief among most parents that a public school education is preferable to that provided by the State. But a more recent development is the tendency for large companies to encourage their employees to send their children to public schools. Some firms (such as Shell) have established insurance schemes to help pay school fees. Others (including Rolls-Royce and the Midland Bank) provide closed scholarships for employees' children. Still others make substantial contributions to the finances of the public schools. The first public school to be established since 1945 (at Milton Abbas, Somerset) was started specifically for industry: for each contribution of £225 per annum, a company is entitled to nominate one boy for the entrance tests. Not only are private firms helping to subsidize the public schools, but they are also encouraging an alteration in the content of the education provided, since the skills required by a technological society are significantly different from those needed by the old classically educated *élite*. Accordingly, the science side of the public schools has been greatly developed.

While companies may obtain their managerial recruits equally from the public and the grammar schools, the public school candidate may receive promotion far more rapidly and more frequently. Furthermore, as C. Wright Mills† suggests, formal qualifications,

* Hollis, C., *Eton*, Hollis & Carter, London, 1960.

† Mills, C. W., *The Power Élite*, Oxford University Press, 1956.

whether educational or professional, cease to be relevant in the higher reaches of industry, and other considerations (such as bearing, manner, accent) come into vital prominence.

Because they think they can take advantage of this situation, an increasing proportion of public school leavers is being attracted into industry. Just after World War II, Rugby sent about one-third of its pupils into private firms, yet in 1957 this had increased to well over half. According to the Public Schools Appointments Board, this reflects the position in the public schools as a whole. As a result, recruitment to the old *élite* occupations, like the Civil Service, has had to widen its basis to include candidates with working-class origins. Once again, however, the advantage lies with public school products: in 1961, out of seventy-eight ambassadors and senior officials in the Foreign Office, sixty-three were ex-public school.

If business is to be efficient and competitive, then clearly class and family nepotism must play a minimal role in personnel selection. Even if it is true today, as Roy Lewis and Rosemary Stewart* suggest, that the public school boy has about ten times as many opportunities to get into management as the general population, and the old Etonian has the most opportunities of all, this is not necessarily going to be a permanent feature of the business world. The larger managerial bureaucracies and corporations have generally adjusted their recruitment policies to cater for the national-wide catchment area available since 1944. Competitive examinations represent the major method of entry into many occupations, professional or otherwise, following the lead given by the Civil Service. If this trend continues, then a complete equality of opportunity may be attained, possibly producing what T. S. Eliot† calls "Jacobinism in education". Eliot argues that an educational system which automatically attempted to sort out every individual so that he reached his optimum level, commensurate with his abilities and aptitudes, would disorganize society. Admittedly it would do much to modify

* Lewis, R., and Stewart, R., *The Boss: The Life and Times of the British Businessman*, Phoenix, London, 1958. See also, Jenkins, C., *Power at the Top*, MacGibbon & Kee, London, 1959.

† Eliot, T. S., *op. cit.*

class consciousness but, on the other hand, it would merely replace classes by intelligence *élites*. This, according to Eliot, could not be termed a qualitative improvement over the existing situation. Dr. Michael Young implicitly makes a similar point in his book, *The Rise of the Meritocracy*.*

The relevance of these remarks to the public schools is simply that, rightly or wrongly, these schools have in the past concentrated on producing a social *élite*. In the future, the public schools may retain their reputation as breeding grounds for an *élite* by changing the emphasis towards intellectual training. No doubt something of the sort would meet with the approval of Lord James, sometime High Master of Manchester Grammar School, who advocates† that the encouragement of an intellectual *élite* should be the primary purpose of the educational system.

At one time the Labour Party, had it been in power, might have considered abolition of the public schools, but this is now unlikely. The schools have shown themselves to be capable of self-reform, and in any case the Labour Party cannot very well deny the liberty of the individual to spend his income as he wishes. The public schools may wither away as redistributive taxation diminishes higher incomes. Yet middle-class parents are manifestly willing to undergo great sacrifices in order that their children may attend fee-paying schools. Moreover, fees can be paid over a period of years, by means of covenants taken out by relatives, insurance policies, etc. And as we have already noted, the public schools still have long waiting lists.

It is not an original idea to suggest a greater degree of integration between the private and the State schools. The 1944 Fleming Committee recommended that the independent schools should offer at least 25 per cent of their places to free pupils entering from the State primary schools. However, the proposal has not been generally adopted, chiefly because local education authorities are unwilling to pay fees for children who could equally well be accommodated in

* Young, M., *The Rise of the Meritocracy*, Thames & Hudson, London, 1958.

† See James, E., *Education for Leadership*.

existing State schools. Opposition also came from working-class parents who feared the unfortunate effects which the public school environment might have on their children.* C. A. R. Crosland,† however, suggests that entry to the public schools should be entirely based on performance in competitive tests, regardless of whether the children had previously been to State or private preparatory schools. In return for accepting this condition, the public schools would be given financial assistance. The ultimate result might be "a more closely knit society" in the words of the 1943 White Paper on Educational Reconstruction.

APPRENTICESHIP AND INDUSTRIAL TRAINING

The Ministry of Labour *Inquiry into Apprenticeship and Training for Skilled Occupations* (1925–6) defines apprenticeship as "the contractual relationship between an employer and a worker under which the employer is obliged to teach the worker". The agreement binding the apprentice to his master is known as an indenture. Although the 1563 Statute of Artificers specified a 7-year period for the apprenticeship, the Ministry of Labour's inquiry indicated that nearly two-thirds of all apprentices serve only a 5-year term, for reasons which will later become obvious. After satisfactory completion of the training, the employer endorses the indentures and hands them to the apprentice. The trade unions accept this endorsed indenture as sufficient for issuing the "skilled ticket" which entitles him to the wages of a craftsman. This arrangement, given here in broad outline, has been the subject of severe criticism for many years, on various grounds, and it will be the aim of subsequent paragraphs to examine these criticisms in greater detail.

Kate Liepmann‡ points out that in the apprenticeship agreement there are not merely two parties, the apprentice and the master, but also a third, namely, the appropriate trade union. Although nowhere explicitly mentioned, the trade unions' interest in apprenticeship

* A problem of this kind was vividly portrayed in Warren Chetham-Strode's play, *The Guinea-pig*.

† Crosland, C. A. R., *op. cit.*

‡ Liepmann, K., *Apprenticeship*, Routledge & Kegan Paul, London, 1960.

springs naturally from their role as protectors of their members' competitive position in the labour market. Clearly nothing would weaken that position more than if the trade could be practised by anyone regardless of training or apprenticeship service. The trade unions, therefore, are diligent in maintaining the scarcity of craftsmen through a restricted quota of apprentices. This alone would be no good, however, if there were other methods of entering a trade—and so trade unions fight against craftsmen of other trades (by demarcation rules) and against non-apprenticed workers (by anti-dilution laws).

Resistance to apprenticeship reform originates chiefly among the unions which, for example, insist that indentures should in most cases cover a 5-year term. Yet many authorities consider that the training required could reasonably be completed in 3 years.* Such is the view of John Wellens,† who argues that for many apprentices the final 2 years are not training at all, but "improvership". Through the increasing complexity of machines and mechanical processes, the greater variety of materials and equipment, the larger number of specialist trades, many of the old crafts have become de-skilled. The result is that so-called "craftsmen" may be doing the same work as semi-skilled men (who are only described as semi-skilled because they have not undergone an apprenticeship). The demand for the old-style craftsman, possessing a number of skills, is now limited to small firms catering for bespoke needs.

A further consideration arises from the P.E.P. publication *Manpower*‡: "If apprenticeship is to appeal to young people entering industry at a time of full employment, the period of training must involve the least possible waste of time."

Craft apprenticeships traditionally end at the age of 21. This was the minimum age of completion specified by the Statute of Artificers, and trade union rules support the *status quo*. The age of 21 is sig-

* An apt comment on this situation came from Lord Hailsham (now Quintin Hogg) in February 1963: "During the war, it took us a matter of months to train a Spitfire pilot. I decline to believe that it takes five years to train a bricklayer."

† Wellens, J., *Education and Training in Industry.*

‡ *Manpower*, Political and Economic Planning, London.

nificant because the general wage structure fixes this as the time when the worker qualifies for adult rates of pay. After becoming 21 years old, too, the apprentice may legally withdraw from his contract. These factors, combined with trade union insistence on a 5-year period, make it almost inevitable that apprenticeships begin at the age of 16. Boys who leave school at 17 are discouraged from becoming apprentices. It is not that the trade union formally objects, but certain difficulties arise when the individual reaches his twenty-first birthday, and many firms prefer to take the easy way out. Yet, as we have seen, more and more children are staying on at school beyond the compulsory minimum age, and those who do leave earliest belong almost invariably to the lowest ability ranges. Hence it is likely that in the future apprenticeship training will have to produce satisfactory craftsmen out of less promising material. This difficulty has been accentuated by the increasing educational opportunities open to working-class boys since the 1944 Education Act, further reducing the likelihood that talented boys need confine their ambitions to craftsman status. About the only consolation here is that if apprentices really do become less able, as a class, then it may take the full 5 years to complete a training which could be achieved in 3 for pupils with normal intelligence!*

Other considerations concern the adequacy or otherwise of the training provided. When the employer endorses the apprentice's indentures, the trade union accepts this as sufficient grounds for issue of the "skilled ticket". The trade union does not worry about the adequacy of the training nor about the craftsman's personal proficiency. Nobody supervises the methods used by the employer to instruct his apprentices. Employers need no special qualifications in order to engage apprentices. Training may be only half complete, so that narrowly specialized or even one-skill men are produced instead of versatile craftsmen. All this could be avoided; for example, there is no lack of external examining bodies against whose standards

* It is interesting to note that there is no upper or lower age limit on apprenticeships in the U.S.A. or Germany; nor is the term of service in those countries as long as it is in Britain at present. See Williams, G., *Apprenticeship in Europe: the Lesson for Britain*, Chapman & Hall, London, 1963.

the apprentice could be evaluated. The City and Guilds Institute publishes syllabuses and holds examinations for over 150 subjects at the craftsman level. For more advanced students, Ordinary and Higher National Certificates are available. In addition there are over 100 national schemes laying down recommended apprenticeship-training procedures for certain industries. On the other hand, the possession of these qualifications is not necessarily indispensable in terms of earning power and promotion. The direct financial rewards of obtaining O.N.C. are not great, especially after the age of 21, since trade unions will not allow craftsmen to earn more than the district rate, regardless of their additional paper qualifications. At best, O.N.C. gives the promise of possible rewards in the distant future.

Apprenticeships are available almost exclusively in the manual crafts alone. According to the P.E.P. *Manpower*,* "The opinion seems to be still quite widely held that if a boy or girl with a reasonably good education is engaged and provided with a desk and a pen, all will be well. This system, or lack of system, is responsible for the most appalling inefficiency and waste of labour." It is in response to criticism of this kind that a National Certificate course in commercial subjects has recently been begun, which incidentally provides opportunities for the more efficient deployment of female labour.

The inescapable conclusion to be drawn from this critical examination of apprenticeship is that it is not fulfilling its aim of providing an adequate number of sufficiently skilled craftsmen to replace and supplement existing workers. At present, apprentice numbers are limited by trade unions, although applicants consistently exceed the vacancies available. In some trades and industries, there is comparatively little distinction today between skilled men, only so described because they have undergone an apprenticeship, and semi-skilled operatives, who may be performing the same machine-minding tasks as their more highly paid colleagues. In the words of Kate Liepmann,† the national interest would be best served if "apprenticeship were divested entirely of the function of preserving

* *Manpower, op. cit.* † Liepmann, K., *op. cit.*

obsolete and restrictive occupational barriers in industry, and became a social institution dealing solely with education and industrial training and extended to the whole working population".

Lastly, a postscript on the use of university graduates in industry. W. S. Robertson has written that "the inadequate use of graduates in U.K. industry . . . is one of several reasons for the fact that, while world trade in manufactured goods increased 2·5 times between 1900–50, British trade increased only 1·6 times". Undoubtedly some of this "inadequate use of graduates" can be attributed to prejudice felt by some managers who have come up the "hard way", namely, promotion from the shop, or factory floor. Industry, of course, cannot afford to be the victim of such irrational prejudice. Fortunately, one of the long-term results of full educational opportunity means that it is no longer necessary for talented individuals to leave school at 15, since they can be wholly supported by the State throughout their period at university. There is unlikely to be a recurrence of such rare cases as Professor Ritchie Calder of Edinburgh University, who was a police-court reporter at 15. The rags-to-riches myth is becoming an even greater illusion as the effects of the 1944 Act make themselves universally felt.

Industry's concern, as regards graduates in general, is that science and technology specialists should be available in even greater quantity. The new universities, the Colleges of Advanced Technology, and some of the bigger technical colleges, should meet the growing demand to some extent. This problem quite likely preoccupies industry far more than the question of apprentice training, since the ever-increasing complexity of manufacturing processes requires highly skilled, versatile staff who can adapt themselves to rapidly changing methods. There is insufficient emphasis on science in the existing universities, according to some authorities, but again the balance between arts and science is being altered by government intervention. In 1958, for example, the Chancellor of the Exchequer announced a 4-year building programme for the universities, costing £60 million, of which two-thirds would be concentrated on the scientific side. This programme, considered the Chancellor, would meet Britain's estimated need for 20,000 newly qualified scientists and engineers annually. Since 1958, further expansion of the universities has been initiated, and recent reports of the University Grants Committee (largely responsible for university finance) show an increasing swing away from the arts.

CHAPTER 5

Leisure

Our paper has to be entertaining; we also incorporate such information and instruction as we think they [the readers] should have. . . . The sort of readers we have find continuous application, except in a really very interesting sex murder, dull; it is too much of an effort to read a whole column, even a short column, of type.

(CECIL KING, Chairman of the *Daily Mirror* Group of Newspapers, in a TV interview)

The shorter working week means more leisure, and yet what the hell is happening?

(ARNOLD WESKER.)

The dictionary defines leisure as freedom from business, occupation, or hurry; unoccupied time or time at one's own disposal. Possibly a more succinct explanation would be in terms of non-productive employment: leisure consists of scholarly and artistic accomplishments, manners, the cultivation of an appropriate style of life. It may seem strange to regard leisure as a problem, but the question is basically a by-product of post-war affluence combined with a general move towards shorter working hours. Even before 1939, many people were concerned lest this leisure time should be "improperly" spent, no doubt recalling the old adage that "Satan finds evil for idle hands to do." There is, of course, a danger that for moralists the "proper" use of leisure implies merely a reflection of their own views on the matter. Be that as it may, it is probably true that in the rush to reduce working hours, those most directly involved have tended to assume that their leisure will look after itself. As

Granville Eastwood* has written, it does seem ironic that trade unions should have struggled hard for generations to gain shorter hours and more adequate pay packets, yet made little or no effort to encourage workers to use their hard-won leisure to best advantage. It was to fill this gap, however inadequately, that Arnold Wesker's *Centre* 42 organization was created, so named after Resolution No. 42 on the Agenda at the 1960 T.U.C. Annual Conference.† Its main purpose was to present cultural entertainments of all kinds to workers in factories, in pubs, or anywhere there might be an audience.

The divorce between work and leisure, which is universally accepted today, is a product of the Industrial Revolution and, more specifically, the emergence of the factory system. Prior to 1750 it was very difficult, if not impossible, for an employer to secure a regular, disciplined labour force. The Protestant ethic made industrialization possible by advocating hard work and abstinence; yet the natural corollary of this belief was an attitude of hostility towards the leisure pursuits of the working classes. The playgrounds of the poor were reduced by the inexorable growth of the towns, and the constant superiority of hard economic pressures produced urban congestion of the most demoralizing kind.‡ Sunday leisure for the manual labourer was limited to the pubs, which only opened for a few hours. In view of the exorbitant hours worked during the initial boom of industrialization, it is surprising that the working classes had any time for leisure at all. As J. H. Plumb§ notes:

* Eastwood, G., "Leisure: The New Problem for Unions", the *Observer*, 8 July 1962.

† The Resolution was worded as follows: "Recognizing the importance of the arts in the life of the community, and noting that the Trade Union movement has participated to only a small extent in the direct promotion of plays, films, music, literature and other forms of expression", the General Council of the T.U.C. was requested to examine the question.

‡ "After 1815 there was an actual worsening of conditions in the rapidly developing factory towns, where houses were being run up wholesale by contractors intent chiefly on cheapness, and the older residential areas were being rapidly converted into slums as the well-to-do citizens moved further out." (From Cole, G. D. H., and Postgate, R., *The Common People 1746–1946*, Methuen, London.)

§ Plumb, J. H., *England in the Eighteenth Century*, Penguin Books, 1950.

> The poorest working men today would have found the lives of their ancestors almost unbearable. The hours of work were fourteen, fifteen, or even sixteen a day, six days a week throughout the year except for Christmas Day and Good Friday. That was the ideal time-table of the industrialists. It was rarely achieved, for the human animal broke down under the burden; and he squandered his time in palliatives—drink, lechery, blood-sports.

For many people, the long hours of labour, in wretched conditions that have been fully documented elsewhere,* produced such desperate fatigue that time spent at home was chiefly time spent in recuperation. Many girls and women, for example, claimed that Sunday (their one day of rest) had to be spent in bed. It was characteristic of the time that even when Jedediah Strutt entertained "the female hands" to "a sumptuous *déjeuner*" to celebrate the passing of the 1832 Reform Act, they had to work off the extra holiday at the rate of an extra hour a day for two weeks.† The entrepreneurs of the Industrial Revolution could be praised for their application and perseverance, their energy, thrift and courage—virtues which are generally regarded as the very epitome of Victorianism. But the other side of the picture is far less attractive, both morally and aesthetically. It is interesting, for example, to consider the energy and perseverance shown by these same entrepreneurs in whittling away the number of holy days on which the Bank of England was closed. These were reduced from 47 in 1761 to about 6, thereby cutting off a further source of leisure time for all sections of the community—leisure time which, to the industrialists, was so much unproductive waste. Despite the fact that Britain pioneered the introduction of official Bank Holidays—they were hailed as "oases of rest and quiet for the ordinary man" when Sir John Lubbock's Act of 1871 was passed—almost every country in the world now has a larger number than we do. England and Wales have six Bank

* For the situation among rural labourers, see George, D., *England in Transition*, Penguin Books, 1953; for the conditions of industrialization, see Pinchbeck, I., *Women Workers and the Industrial Revolution, 1750–1850*, Routledge & Kegan Paul, London, 1930; also Thompson, D., *England in the Nineteenth Century, 1815–1914*, Penguin Books, 1950.

† Quoted in Fitton, R. S., and Wadsworth, A. P., *The Strutts and the Arkwrights, 1758–1830*, Manchester University Press, 1959.

Holidays, Scotland has five: every other nation in the Commonwealth and every country in Europe surpasses this figure.*

The notion of taking a formal holiday grew up originally among the wealthy classes who went to health spas such as Bath and Cheltenham in order to take the waters. Because they had to stay at these places for some time, amusements had to be provided for them, like the concerts sponsored by Nash. Various contributory factors accelerated the spread of the holiday as a social institution. For example, just as the Industrial Revolution brought with it an increasing degree of geographical and occupational movement, so this was in turn made possible by the development of mechanized modes of transport and communication during the nineteenth century. The railways, which for the first time made cheap travel a reality for the poorer classes, were particularly important in this connection. Higher standards of living among all sections of the community have facilitated the growth of industries catering for private transport in this century: the bicycle, the motor-cycle, the car. The increasing availability of these modes of conveyance not only created new forms of leisure in themselves (cycle touring, car outings, even car cleaning and maintenance), but also largely promoted the growth of the suburbs, since people could now live at greater distances from their work. The suburbs offer far wider scope for the more satisfactory use of leisure time than did the crowded collection of narrow slums built in the shadow of the factories. If nothing else, the density of houses per acre in the suburbs is generally sufficient to allow a garden area for each property.

Apart from the steady reduction in working hours brought about by periodic factory legislation in the nineteenth century, there has been growing acceptance of the idea of a paid holiday each year for all workers, usually a minimum of 2 weeks. This has been justified on the grounds that if people are expected to work regular hours, they ought to have regular times set aside for holidays too. Moreover,

* France and Germany have ten full national holidays; Belgium and Sweden have eleven; Italy and Spain have thirteen. Apart from Kenya (with eight), no country in the Commonwealth has fewer than nine Bank Holidays. In the U.S.A., where the number of Bank Holidays fluctuates from State to State, the average citizen gets twice as many official holidays as a Scotsman.

the holiday is thought to act as a restorative force and even indirectly to result in increased productivity. In the 25 years that have elapsed since the passage of the Holidays With Pay Act, a fortnight's annual vacation has come to be acknowledged as the minimum standard. Here again, although this has been a major advance, Britain is left behind by other countries: for example, the introduction of a fourth week's paid holiday was one of the issues at stake during a serious French coal strike in the early part of 1963. However, the post-war period has certainly seen an enormous growth in what might be called the holiday habit. Two-thirds of the population now take some form of vacation away from home each year.* Throughout the industrialized world the same pattern is appearing. Increased mechanization is allowing fewer workers to produce more goods, and there is absolutely no sign at all that this trend is going to be reversed. Already there are some signs that, during the next decade, 4 weeks' holiday with pay could easily become an accepted minimum standard in our industries. There is a strong tendency for middle-class habits (in, for example, family planning) to filter down to the working class, and even now many middle-class occupations and professions typically enjoy 3 or 4 weeks' vacation.

* This figure takes no account of class differences. Richard Hoggart (*The Uses of Literacy*, Chatto & Windus, London, 1957) says of the working-class man: "Nor does he travel a great deal, in spite of the great changes in transport during the last fifty years. There are 'chara' trips, football excursions and perhaps an annual holiday, and occasional train trips to the funeral or wedding of some member of a branch of the family. . . . Before he married, he may possibly have gone to the Continent, or seen some distant parts of England by push-bike; he probably travelled a great deal during war-service or National Service. But after marriage, and if we leave aside the occasions just mentioned, the speed and extent of his travel are not much different from what they would have been thirty years ago." To some extent, this unduly pessimistic picture is endorsed in a comprehensive survey of Derby (Cauter, T., and Downham, J. S., *The Communication of Ideas, A Study of Contemporary Influences on Urban Life*, Chatto & Windus, London, 1954), which indicates that, among those interviewed, one in four of the middle classes had made a journey out of Derby in 1952, compared with only 10 per cent of the working classes (day or 2-day trips were excluded). Today, this sharp class differential has probably been modified: when the working-class family takes a holiday, it may often choose to visit relatives (which is not only cheaper but more homely), and if they go abroad, they go to Ostend rather than the Riviera.

The use of leisure time can be discussed either from the viewpoint of age or from that of class. Either way, it is important to remember that to meet the need for leisure pursuits in a prosperous market economy, leisure has been commercialized. There are now powerful specialists in fulfilling the mass demand for spare-time activities in the shape of the cinema, TV, newspapers, football, etc. These large-scale enterprises—inspired not so much by philanthropy as by the profit motive—are often important media of communication for certain ideas and beliefs. For example, there is a decided tendency to place a higher value on "active" as opposed to "passive" pursuits, and the Duke of Edinburgh accordingly runs a campaign for active leisure and it has even been suggested* that the Government should legislate for compulsory games among the working class (on the analogy suggested by the public schools). Apart from the fact that the latter proposal is, of course, impracticable, the distinction between active and passive leisure is more subtle than it at first appears. The apparent dichotomy may be the product of middle-class social commentators, who look down on working-class leisure occupations primarily for status reasons. If middle-class leisure is more active, it may be because the middle class is largely engaged in sedentary jobs, and therefore needs the exercise. If, as is the case, the middle class indulges in sporting activities (as distinct from spectatorship) more often than the working class, this need not reflect any fundamental difference in outlook, but merely normal physical limitations: the manual labourer gets sufficient exercise from his work.

Patterns of leisure in contemporary Britain are heavily influenced by the ubiquitous teenager. During this period, which Dr. Mark Abrams† calls the first of the five ages of leisure, a high proportion of non-working time is spent outside the home and in the company of the teenagers' own age groups—at cinemas, dance-halls, evening classes, clubs, cafés, attending mass spectator sports, taking part in team games, walking and cycling. In recent years, the period between

* Sir Charles Darwin, F.R.S., in the *New Scientist*.

† Abrams, M., "The Five Ages of Leisure", the *Observer*, 19 November 1960.

the minimum school-leaving age and the attainment of maturity has attracted the attention not only of those authorities concerned with the welfare of the adolescent, but also of the economic interests in society. It is now possible for a school-leaver to earn a reasonably good wage. Dr Abrams* estimated that, in 1959, the average male teenager spent 71*s*. 6*d*. a week, and the average girl 54*s*. 0*d*. "Britain's five million teenagers, after meeting their State and family obligations and after putting aside approximately £70 millions as true savings, spent £830 millions, or slightly over 5 per cent of the national total consumer expenditure." This economic revolution of the inarticulate—the C and D secondary modern streams who are suddenly faced with the task of spending about £3 a week—has naturally been catered for by the commercial enterprises which know that a sizeable proportion of the national income goes into the pockets of young earners. As a result, teenagers have been transformed into a highly self-conscious stratum in society. As Dr. Abrams† remarks:

> By and large one can generalize by saying that the quite large amount of money at the disposal of Britain's average teenager is spent mainly on dress and on goods which form the nexus of teenage gregariousness outside the home. In other words, this is distinctive teenage spending for distinctive teenage ends in a distinctive teenage world.

One of the most vital factors affecting adolescence is the emergence of heterosexual urges, and there is considerable evidence to suggest that puberty is occurring up to 6 months earlier with each generation. At present, its onset can take place at any age between 8 and 16, but higher standards of living and greater security have significantly lowered this critical age. Perhaps part of the cause, too, is what David Holbrook‡ calls "a completely packaged Brave New World of sexual awareness, from commercial sources". T. R. Fyvel§ agrees that "sex has never received such massive publicity as today, from the ubiquitous underclothes advertisements to the incessant erotic gossip

* Abrams, M., *Teenage Consumer Spending in 1959* (Part II), London Press Exchange Ltd., 1961.

† Abrams, M., *op. cit.*

‡ Holbrook, D., "What Is Sex After All?" *Spectator*, 14 October 1960.

§ Fyvel, T. R., *The Insecure Offenders.* Chatto & Windus, London, 1961.

in the popular press". Undoubtedly it is true that there is far more freedom in both the discussion and the performance of sex* than, say, 50 years ago, although, as a causal factor in the onset of puberty, it has almost certainly been overrated by Fyvel and Holbrook. What is surprising, reading Fyvel's impressionistic account† of the atypical Teddy Boy era, is the youthfulness of the participants in the kind of behaviour described. By the time a boy is 15—and for a girl the equivalent age is about a year earlier, since girls mature quicker than boys—he is ready for sex. The Teddy Boy movement, by giving group sanction to complete sexual freedom, enabled him to get it. By extension, it might even be argued that the whole

* Some interesting class variants in sexual behaviour have been revealed in the U.S.A. by Kinsey. A lower-level male may have intercourse with dozens of girls he casually encounters and not kiss any of them, at least more than superficially. By contrast, the comparatively well-educated male from the higher strata of society engages in frequent tongue-kissing with many girls, and yet no doubt many of these same males would recoil at the thought of sharing a drinking-glass; lower-class people consider tongue-kissing to be filthy and unsanitary. Upper-class couples are more experimental in their love-making (perhaps because they have higher I.Q.s and more imagination): they make love in the nude (a thought which appals many in the lower level) and they occasionally make love in the light (regarded by the lower strata as an even more appalling and indecent arrangement). Kinsey also suggests that masturbation is more common among the upper classes—possibly because they are inhibited in their relations with the opposite sex. In some low-class communities, it was impossible to find a single male who had not, by the time he was 17, had sexual relations: the boy destined to become a semi-skilled worker was fifteen times as likely to have intercourse by the time he was 16 as the boy destined to enter the "upper white-collar" category. Pre-marital intercourse, indeed, was regarded as a normal and natural occurrence for males at the lower social levels; and Hollingshead found corroboratory evidence in Elmtown that "sex mores were violated far more frequently" by adolescents in the two lower classes than in the middle and upper strata. How far the foregoing is applicable to this country is, of course, a matter for conjecture, but it seems likely that, having adopted so many features of the American way of life, Britain may also have inculcated at least some aspects of American sexual behaviour. See Kinsey, A. C., Pomeroy, W. B., and Martin, C. E., *Sexual Behaviour in the Human Male*, W. B. Saunders Co., Philadelphia, U.S.A., 1948; same authors, plus Gebhard, P. H., *Sexual Behaviour in the Human Female*, W. B. Saunders Co., Philadelphia, U.S.A., 1953; Hollingshead, A. B., *Elmtown's Youth*, John Wiley, New York, U.S.A., 1949.

† Fyvel, T. R., *op. cit.*

working-class attitude to precocious sexual promiscuity would encourage an uninhibited approach for working-class youths. This is the kind of vicious stereotype upon which is founded, despite the complete lack of reliable evidence, the frequent criticism of teenage morals that one finds in the popular press and elsewhere. In the minds of parents, the stereotype has gained a particularly powerful hold. It is associated chiefly with what are believed to be (again with no basis of concrete facts) working-class habits. "If I go out with a boy who's in the C.N.D.", said one 17-year-old girl quoted by Godfrey Smith,* "my parents go mad and lie awake worrying till I come home. They equate Ban-the-Bomb with every kind of moral depravity. But if I go out with, say, a young Liberal, I can come in at 4 a.m. and they will sleep on quite peacefully." Kinsey,† in the U.S.A., has suggested that whereas middle-class parents put very strict obstacles in the way of overt sexual satisfaction for their children, working-class parents are much more lax and unconcerned. These conclusions have limited relevance in this country, where the advisability of pre-marital experiments in order to prove compatibility is now freely discussed in all sections of the community, regardless of class.‡

Gorer§ concludes: "The younger generation—those under 24—are just as strict in their views of desirable and undesirable sexual behaviour as their elders. There seems to be every reason to believe that the sexual morals of the English have changed very little in the present century." Undoubtedly the whole issue of teenage sexual behaviour,|| and teenage behaviour in general, has been absurdly

* Smith, G., "Two Worlds: A Stranger in the House", *Sunday Times*, 12 January 1963.

† Kinsey, A. C., Pomeroy, W. B., and Martin, C. E., *op. cit.*

‡ Viz. the *Reith Lectures* by Professor G. M. Carstairs, November 1962: "In our society the rules governing sexual behaviour are already changing and may yet change even more. . . . Perhaps in another thirty years contraceptive methods will be quite safe; and perhaps by that time we shall look back smilingly at the alarm which talk of pre-marital sex caused among us at this time."

§ Gorer, G., *Exploring English Character*, Cresset Press, London, 1955.

|| One little girl, quoted by David Holbrook (*op. cit.*), said: "If we don't begin to get to know each other now, when we *need* to get to know each other we shan't know anything about each other!"

over-publicized. Perhaps one of the most appropriate observations relating to the problem has been made by Alderman George Stokes, Mayor of Wednesbury, Staffordshire, when a Roman Catholic organization established that Wednesbury teenagers' chief hobby was courting. Courting, said Alderman Stokes, was an international hobby not peculiar to Wednesbury, and to suggest that was all the youngsters did in their leisure time was bunkum.*

How, then, do teenagers occupy their non-working hours? A large proportion of the answer to this question can be obtained by examining the pattern of teenage expenditure. According to Dr. Abrams,† it appears that the average working boy pays his parents roughly 35*s.* 0*d.*, and the average working girl 25*s.* 0*d.* a week for board and lodging. Of the remainder, with tax and National Insurance taken into account, 31 per cent of the average boy's expenditure goes on drinks, cigarettes, and entertainment admissions, and nearly 40 per cent of the average girl's expenditure goes on clothes, shoes, and cosmetics. Since the word "drinks" has just been mentioned, it ought to be explained that very little is actually spent on alcoholic liquor. The latest figures, says Dr. Abrams, "show that less than 40 per cent of male teenagers take any alcoholic drink as often as once a week. Among girls, the abstainers are even more numerous—less than 10 per cent have any alcohol as often as once a week." Moreover, the definition of "teenager" adopted by Dr. Abrams for the purposes of his survey referred to "those young people who have reached the age of 15 but are not yet 25 years of age and are unmarried". If the 15 to 20 group had been taken separately, then no doubt the alcohol consumption and spending figures would be even less than Dr. Abrams quotes.‡

* Report in the *Sunday Times*, 8 November 1959; quoted in Fletcher, R., *The Family and Marriage*, Penguin Books, 1962.

† Abrams, M., *Teenage Consumer Spending in 1959* (Part II), London Press Exchange Ltd., 1961.

‡ Before 1900, the consumption of alcohol was rising; afterwards, it began to fall and since the early thirties the consumption of alcohol per head has been less than half what it was in 1900. There is much less violent drunkenness nowadays, although among the working class the view that "A man needs 'is pint" still prevails: drink is regarded as a man's natural prerogative, so long as he keeps within the bounds of moderation." See Prest, A. R., with

Of the 5 million or so young people aged between 15 and 20 in Britain, about one-fifth are either still receiving full-time education at school or college, or else are in the armed forces. For present purposes, this proportion can be considered as playing only a very minor role in the affluent teenager market. It is the remaining 80 per cent, the mostly working-class majority of 3 million boys and girls in this age group, which make up the composite picture of the teenage consumer. As Dr. Abrams* illuminatingly points out, the average real weekly wages of young people in the 15 to 21 age group were over 50 per cent higher in 1960 than before the war. In addition, because parents are more prosperous, their children can now keep a much higher proportion of their earnings to spend on themselves. It might well be the case, therefore, that a dustman's daughter would have more actual pocket-money than her father. With teenage spending running at an estimated £900 million a year, it is not surprising that whole industries cater exclusively for this clientele: records and record-players, soft drinks, magazines, distinctive clothes, motor-cycles and scooters, and cosmetics. T. R. Fyvel† concludes that

> working-class adolescents are being incessantly persuaded to spend much of their money on a comparatively narrow range of goods, mostly mass-produced. . . . The need to maintain such spending has also led to a concentrated barrage of advertising on the youth market, and to magazines, films, radio and television shows specially angled to attract youth.

The emphasis on the working class is not misplaced, for "The aesthetic of the teenage market is essentially a working-class aesthetic", in Dr. Abrams' phrase.‡ In other words, just as middle-class and working-class adolescents used to be differentiated by the comparative poverty of the latter, so today it is the middle-class

---

Adams, A. A., *Consumer's Expenditure in the United Kingdom 1900–1919*, Cambridge University Press, 1954; Commissioners of Customs and Excise, *Report*, 1951–1952 (Cmd. 8727), H.M.S.O.

* Abrams, M., *op. cit.* † Fyvel, T. R., *op. cit.*

‡ Abrams, M., *op. cit.*

youth who is poor and his working-class counterpart who is characterized by his affluence and his own peculiar spending habits.

In his novel *Absolute Beginners*, Colin MacInnes* has one of his characters say:

> As for the boys and girls, the dear young absolute beginners, I sometimes feel that if they only knew this fact, this very simple fact, namely how powerful they really are, then they could rise up overnight and enslave the old taxpayers, the whole damn lot of them—toupets and falsies and rejuvenators and all.

But in reality the teenagers are not so powerful, either economically or otherwise, because they do not constitute a permanently stable group. Their tastes change very rapidly, and each year a proportion of their number defects in order to get married. As a result, the commercial interests geared to the demands of the teenage market must find new ways to attract the support of the emerging 15-year-olds, and this means a constant search for new fashions, new gimmicks, new sensations, most of which derive from the U.S.A. because there the teenage market is so much bigger. Nevertheless, some factors remain constant. The pop musical market, for example, has become an established ritual of so-called "stars" coming and going at regular intervals. The fact that most of these pop singers† are male reflects nothing more than the overwhelming dominance of the young male in the 15 to 20 age group. He is numerically stronger than girls, he earns more, and so disposes of about two-thirds of teenage spending-money.

One of the negative implications of the "youth culture" described by T. R. Fyvel‡ is, according to him, that it "draws young people still further away from their families and homes", and he also talks about "the new generation of indifferent parents, and their children who roam around the streets". This point of view is hotly contested

* MacInnes, C., *Absolute Beginners*.

† Fyvel, T. R., *op. cit.*, describes pop singers as "shrewdly manufactured idols of the youth culture—young men fabulously successful yet explicitly publicized as being of working-class origin, and in fact, except for their money and success, like any ordinary youngster who spends his money on pop music."

‡ Fyvel, T. R., *op. cit.*

by Ronald Fletcher* who remarks that, when thinking of the period before industrialization, "The picture of the large, contented family practising its manifold recreations in the cosy fire-lit homestead is itself something of a caricature". Nowadays, the scope of activities for leisure hours has not only increased, but so has the actual opportunity for participating in leisure: Ronald Fletcher asks, "Do brothers and sisters never join the same social clubs, church clubs, scout troops, guide troops? . . . Do families never gather at the end of the day around the fateful face of television? Do they not argue over the respective merits of 'Wagon Train', 'Sunday Night at the London Palladium' . . .?" T. R. Fyvel and Ronald Fletcher are clearly proponents of totally contradictory attitudes, but probably the situation is neither as grim as the one paints it, nor as beautiful as described by the other.† Assuming that the teenage consumer market is calculated to appeal to teenagers and to nobody else, then it follows quite naturally that their parents will be, if not actively hostile,‡ then passively bewildered. It is scarcely surprising, therefore, that parents and children find it difficult to communicate.

From the moment they marry, set up a home, and have children, most young working-class couples have to become accustomed to entirely new spending habits, a transition for which they have usually not been well prepared. Indeed, they have to make the

* Fletcher, R., *op. cit.*

† So far as working-class families are concerned, leisure activities revolve round the home much more than, say, 50 years ago. As Willmott and Young noted of Bethnal Green, "The spread of the five-day week has created the 'week-end', a new term and a new experience for the working man." Material affluence has also been a vital factor here, for as Dr. Mark Abrams notes, "Once, the working-class husband sought to escape from the crowded shabbiness of his home to the warmth and conviviality of 'pubs' or the club rooms of voluntary associations. . . . But now, as far as shabbiness and smartness are concerned, the boot is on the other foot; so the new man stays at home." See Young, M., and Willmott, P., *Family and Kinship in East London*, Routledge & Kegan Paul, London, 1957; Abrams, M., "The Home-centred Society", *Listener*, 26 November 1959.

‡ "Young people have never been under more heavy fire; their manners, their spending habits, their love of modern dancing and modern music, have all been the subject of abuse" (Brew, J. M., *Youth and Youth Groups*, Faber & Faber, London, 1957). It is not surprising that many adolescents reacted violently against this.

change twice over: once when they get married, even though the wife (as is the typical case in the middle class, too) still continues at work; and again when the wife has to give up her employment in order to have a child. This latter change is generally the more drastic of the two, since the couple may have acclimatized themselves to a standard of living based on their joint income. Not only does the income of one of the partners disappear, but also there is another mouth to feed. However, for all social classes this is the second main stage of life, extending from the wedding to the period when the children are entering their teens. Today, nearly 70 per cent of young women and 55 per cent of young men are married before the age of 25. Family building is, in turn, concentrated into a comparatively short period. Only 10 per cent of all babies are born to women aged 35 or more. In these circumstances, says Dr. Abrams,* young married people must perforce spend their leisure time largely at home. Their recreational activities tend to consist of watching TV, reading, gardening, do-it-yourself,† listening to the radio, knitting and sewing.

About 85 per cent of these young households have a TV set (compared with 65 per cent as the overall figure for the country as a whole), and it seems that the average young couple spends almost 20 hours weekly watching programmes. By contrast, the average adult aged over 34 spends little more than 10 hours per week at the TV set; this is, on the face of it, surprising, since one would normally expect older people to gain more enjoyment from this essentially passive form of leisure. Class differences in the ownership of TV sets have almost been ironed out, although this was not true in, say, 1954, when there was a strong correlation between set ownership and weekly income. This was presumably due to the higher price of

* Abrams, M., "The Five Ages of Leisure", the *Observer*, 19 November 1960.

† "It is primarily in the home that the worker now has his greatest opportunities for exercising and enjoying his craftmanship", according to Dr. Mark Abrams ("The Home-centred Society", *Listener*, 26 November 1959). The tendency for so-called skilled occupations to become routinized or reduced to little more than machine-minding has been noted elsewhere in this book.

receivers at that time, coupled with the status-conferring prestige to be gained from possession of a set. Also, there was once a close correlation between TV set ownership and educational attainment. In this case the relationship was curvilinear: that is, those with elementary education and those with further education had a low proportion of sets; in the middle was a high proportion of those with secondary education. To some extent, an above-average educational attainment could itself be correlated with above-average income and therefore with TV set ownership. This relationship is virtually meaningless today, when a TV receiver is an item of furniture on furniture on the same terms as the radio.

Watching television is definitely not a young person's choice of pastime, for reasons which are fundamentally not surprising. As T. R. Fyvel* penetratingly remarks, "There is little point in sitting with your girl in front of some living-room television screen. Either adults are present, in which case you are not at ease, or else, if you are alone with a girl, there are better things to do than to watch telly." Occasionally, too, the teenager is able to offer quite accurate and forceful criticism of the general atmosphere created by TV. One youth is quoted† as saying: "It's all those advertisements. They're something horrible. You see a bloke with a gun just going to shoot somebody, and next thing you get 'OMO adds Brightness', and when it starts again you see the police are already in the room."

It is this sort of suggestion which raises the question of the social impact of television. What changes has it brought, if any, to the lives of the British people? Certainly it has altered the domestic habits of countless families. On the one hand it now matches the weather as a staple topic of conversation, both inside the family circle and outside, while on the other it does encourage the family to remain at home during their leisure time. This view, of course, contradicts the pessimism of those who postulate the continuing dissolution of the family under present-day circumstances. Almost any publican will testify to the increasing tendency of his customers to take their bottles home rather than spend their evenings in the

* Fyvel, T. R., *op. cit.* † Fyvel, T. R., *op. cit.*

pub. Yet the very universality of television makes it all the more open to attack.

> The *panem et circenses* school of criticism . . . makes television accountable in whole or in part for most of the commonly deplored social ills of the times: for the prevalence, and sometimes even for the techniques, of juvenile violence; for conformity and passivity of outlook; for neglect of parental responsibilities; for lack of discrimination in matters of taste; for the cult of personality at the expense of ideas and principles; for improvident hire purchase commitments; for materialistic standards of judgment. On the other hand, commentators of a different kidney have found it responsible for . . . the appearance of a better-informed public opinion, for a stimulation of interest in what is going on in the world; for an enrichment of home life.*

A recent survey† of married adults aged between 25 and 34 showed that in the 7 days preceding the interview, a quarter of them had not been outside the house apart from going to work or doing some shopping. Husbands within the same group were a little less housebound. In an average week, nearly half had been out for a drink at the pub or working men's club, and during the football season about 10 per cent had gone to watch a match. But with more and more families, whatever their social origins, assuming the responsibilities of house ownership, the home is likely to take up a major proportion of the husband's (and the wife's) leisure time. As Willmott and Young‡ noted:

> Two-thirds of the people in Woodford live in privately-owned houses. For the men, their houses provide almost endless opportunities for work. Cleaning windows, washing-down walls, interior painting, repairing house and furniture form an annual routine to set against a 5-year plan of improvement and conversion. Why this pre-occupation with the house? The most obvious reason is sheer pride of ownership. . . . He can identify himself and his house and feel that as he improves it he is also in a sense adding to his own stature, in the eyes of his wife and his children, his neighbours and himself. A second reason is that the house is an opportunity for using and developing his capacity as a craftsman. The work of the day, in office or factory, may be becoming

* Supplement on Television 1936–1961, *The Times,* 20 November 1961.

† Quoted in Abrams, M., "The Five Ages of Leisure", the *Observer,* 19 November 1960.

‡ Young, M., and Willmott, P., *Family and Class in a London Suburb,* Routledge & Kegan Paul, London, 1960.

more and more boring. To compensate for this, the work of the night or week-end may be becoming psychologically more and more rewarding. The third reason is that the house is regarded as a sort of business."

One informant is quoted as saying: "I got an estimate for a decorating job recently, just to see what it would cost, and they wanted £34."

As they pass their middle thirties, so the compulsive home ties on parents begin to slacken. They cease to have children, and their existing children either start to go out to work or, if still at school, are regarded as being capable of looking after themselves in the evenings and at weekends. For the married woman, this loosening of the domestic ties does not mean increased leisure: she characteristically uses the additional time in order to work. About 40 per cent of all married women aged between 35 and 44 are under employment somewhere. The comparable figure for younger married women is about 20 per cent. A recent T.U.C. document* emphasized that "women are a permanent part of the labour force. . . . Even if they do get married and have children they will give a large part of their lives to work in industry, commerce, and the services."

Some of the extra money acquired from these two sources—wives and children at work—is spent on extending the home-centred leisure activities acquired during the early years of marriage. Gardening and do-it-yourself projects become more elaborate and require more expensive equipment; there is a little more home entertaining; TV viewing takes place in front of a bigger screen. But, says Dr. Abrams,† the most important change is towards leisure activities outside the home. More time is spent in pubs, in church, in visiting friends, in holidays away from home. Less than 30 per cent of adults in the 25 to 34 age group live in households possessing a car, whereas for adults aged between 35 and 44 the equivalent proportion is 40 per cent.

The fourth main stage in the development of leisure activities concerns the age group 45 to 64. In such households there are few

* The Industrial Charter for Women, prepared by the Women's Advisory Committee of the Trades Union Congress; details from the *Daily Telegraph*, 16 April 1963.

† Abrams, M., *op. cit.*

young children—in all families where the housewife is aged between 45 and 64, only 18 per cent contain a child under school-leaving age —and on average the family contains two earners. Of these latter, the subsidiary earner is usually an adolescent, but 20 per cent of all married women in the age group 45 to 64 go out to work. Whatever the source of the income, however, this period is the most prosperous in the whole family life. On the other hand, this comparatively greater affluence coincides with slackening physical energy. Thus the whole period is typically characterized by a marked increase in home-based leisure activities, such as eating and drinking, or watching television.

The final phase of life, so far as leisure is concerned, begins at 65, the age when most people retire, their incomes drop sharply, their time available for leisure increases markedly but their physical and mental skills and energy are waning. There are 6 million in this category. Of the 2,350,000 men only 20 per cent are still at work, and of the 3,650,000 women only one-third have a husband. Nearly a quarter of the whole depend on National Assistance to supplement their pensions. Against this background, it is scarcely surprising that the leisure occupations of the old chiefly take the form of inexpensive or even free pursuits. In an average week, only 5 per cent go to a cinema (despite the fact that many cinemas have special prices for old age pensioners) and only 15 per cent visit a pub. In Bethnal Green, one of the most often-quoted reasons given by old people for giving up their long association with the pub was that although they could afford to buy the odd pint for themselves, they could not afford to stand a round for their friends and acquaintances. Rather than face the humiliation of having to refuse, they stayed away.

Only 40 per cent of people over 65 take a holiday away from home. Since no more than 15 per cent live in households with a car, occasional drives to the seaside or the country are rare. Wireless is still more common than TV, and on a typical afternoon the most frequent pastime is having a sleep. The older generation reads fewer magazines and newspapers than the rest of the adult population (this is partly a reflection of economic pressures, partly the result of declining powers of concentration). Their contacts with the outside world, such as they are, take a more parochial, direct and personal form. Most of them are visited quite frequently by nearby relatives, friends and social workers (either voluntary or professional). Indeed, as Dr. Abrams notes* the satisfaction and pleasure to be gained from retirement depend heavily on these personal relationships. Part of the difficulty lies in the attitude to retirement which regards it as a period of decrepitude leading merely to the graveyard. This view is gradually being eliminated; according to Ronald Fletcher:† "If old people could be materially secure, there is no reason why the period of retirement should not be regarded in a positive constructive way, as a time when many interests and activities, for which there has been neither time nor opportunity earlier, can now be undertaken."

Of the mass media of communication, we have already noted how the impact of television is largely lost on young people, but has gained a relatively firm hold on married couples with home ties. Yet exactly the opposite situation applies to the cinema, which is characteristically a young person's form of entertainment. That this has been appreciated by the film-makers themselves is shown by the large proportion of productions which specifically cater for teenagers. In the country as a whole, the average number of attendances for the total population in 1952 was twenty-seven, which was higher than the U.S.A. average. Expenditure on the cinema in that year was nearly 3*s.* 0*d.* a week for every family in the country, spread over nearly 4600 cinemas. Some of the latter have since closed or been converted for alternative uses in the face of severe competition from other forms of leisure. As Cauter and Downham's survey of Derby‡ indicates, the group going most frequently to the cinema is that composed of working-class people aged between 16 and 24. Eighty-seven per cent of this section were said to attend the pictures regularly, compared with only 25 per cent of the 65–69 age group. No doubt the high rate of cinema attendance for young people can be partially explained by the fact that the cinema itself performs both manifest and latent functions: the former is the attraction of the film, while

* Abrams, M., *op. cit.* † Fletcher, R., *op. cit.*
‡ Cauter, T., and Downham, J. S., *op. cit.*

the latter is summed up in T. R. Fyvel's remark,* "sex on the screen and a good deal of it in the auditorium too".

As regards newspapers, two facts stand out. First, there has been an enormous and continuing increase in the circulation of both national and provincial dailies since 1945. Between 1937 and 1947, national and provincial dailies increased their sales from 17,800,000 to 28,503,000, while during the same period the circulation of Sunday papers swelled from 15,500,000 to 29,300,000.† In the following six years, Sunday papers reached a peak of 31,700,000. As the authors of the Derby survey‡ comment: "Even when allowance is made for rising prices, we bought more reading material in 1952 than in 1948 (when expenditure was almost exactly double that of 10 years earlier)." If Napoleon thought Britain was a nation of shopkeepers, any Martian might be excused for thinking that we are a nation of newspaper readers. The estimated number of copies of daily papers issued per 1000 of the population is higher in the United Kingdom than in any other country in the world. According to the 1953 Hulton Survey,§ two out of four read three or more Sunday papers. Daily papers are produced now at the rate of two copies for each household in the country. This enormous sale has its class connotations, of course. The so-called "posh" papers (like the *Sunday Times*, the *Observer*, the *Guardian*, *The Times*) are confined to a readership mostly in the top echelons of society, "top" according to the criteria of wealth or occupation or educational attainment (viz. the advertising campaign based on the slogan, "Top People Read *The Times*"). At the other end of the scale are the *Daily Mirror*‖ and the *Daily Sketch*, and the *News of the World*. The latter, although well past the peak which it attained in the middle fifties, still claims

* Fyvel, T. R., *op. cit.*

† Figures from Royal Commission on the Press: *Report* (Cmd. 7700), H.M.S.O., London, 1949.

‡ Cauter, T., and Downham, J. S., *op. cit.*

§ *Hulton Readership Survey, 1952–1955*, Hulton Press, London.

‖ The circulation of the *Daily Mirror*, in April 1963, was 4,660,445 copies. It is owned by the International Publishing Corporation, Ltd. (Chairman: Cecil King), largest publishing house in the world, whose other properties include the *Sunday Mirror*, *The Sun*, *The People*, the Fleetway Magazine Group, and the journals formerly published independently by Odham's.

the largest readership of any Sunday newspaper, and according to the Hulton Readership Survey, it is read in at least half of all households in the working-class and poor categories of society (constituting 70 per cent of the population in the Hulton classification), and in a third of all lower middle-class homes.

Secondly, despite the manifest increase in the market for newspapers, the harsh economies of the industry make it impossible for a publication to survive unless it has a very large readership. As long ago as 1946, Francis Williams* thought it likely that "to exist, a modern national paper in Britain must secure a circulation of at the very least close upon a million and a half and preferably one of over two millions (which means that it must regularly be of a kind to appeal to between five and a quarter million and seven million people)." It is likely that these figures would be much higher today, since rising prices have made it that much more difficult to run a paper on a profitable basis. The tendency provoked by newspaper economics is for ownership of publications to be concentrated in fewer hands as publishers become more and more conscious of the extent to which the economies of scale operate in their industry. The trend has been met with misgiving in some quarters because it may lead to a monopoly in news presentation. As it is, the overwhelming majority of newspapers are either Conservative or independent Conservative. Only one has formal connection with the Labour Party, for which over 12½ million people voted in the 1964 General Election. Yet as the figures† in Table 16 show, the *Daily Herald* (now replaced by *The Sun*) only attracted the allegiance of 21 per cent of Labour supporters, compared with the 42 per cent who read the *Daily Mirror*. Apart from this, newspaper readership is closely correlated with political partisanship, at least for the two main parties; the significance of the *Daily Mirror* and the *Express* for the Liberals does not need any underlining.

The only two newspapers at present issued in this country which do not rely heavily on the support of advertising are the *Daily Worker*

* Williams, F., *Press, Parliament and People*, Heinemann, London, 1946.

† From Butler, D. E., "The Floating Voter", *Sunday Times*, 17 March 1963.

TABLE 16

Newspaper	Party supporters as proportion of total readership (%)		
	Conservatives	Labour	Liberals
Daily Mirror	16	42	30
Daily Express	36	24	32
Daily Mail	25	11	18
Daily Herald	3	21	6
Daily Telegraph	14	3	4
Total	100	100	100

and the *New Daily*.* Both are sponsored by minority movements prepared to make a loss so long as they can still maintain an outlet for their opinions and policies. For other papers, the size of their circulation is alone not enough to guarantee a profit for the publisher. For this he must rely on the supplementary income gained from advertisers, and the constant search for advertising is itself the crux of success or failure for those newspapers with marginal circulations (between one and two million copies). The *News Chronicle*, for example, was bound to collapse because its circulation was so small. Because its circulation was small, it could not recoup its losses by charging high fees for advertising, nor were potential advertisers particularly keen to buy space. And, because the paper lacked advertising, people would not buy it. Circles seldom come as vicious as this, and the end was almost inevitable. It remains to be seen whether the same fate will overtake the other publications, daily or Sunday, in the same dilemma. The problem does not concern the "quality" newspapers so much, since they are able to prove that although their circulations are small, their readership consists largely of people with high incomes who are consequently able to exert a

* In April 1963 the *New Daily* celebrated its third anniversary by announcing that in a year's time the paper should be well on the way towards achieving its declared aim of overhauling the circulation of the *Guardian*. This prediction was not fulfilled.

good deal of spending power. The *Daily Express** combines the advantages of both a very high circulation and a large proportion (it claims) of upwardly-mobile, go-ahead, dynamic young readers who are deeply conscious of status—it is not for nothing that the *Express* was the first newspaper in this country to carry the Ford "Be a Two-car Family" advertisement.

One of the indirectly beneficent side-effects of contemporary affluence noted by J. K. Galbraith is that culture suddenly becomes within the economic reach of more people. The magnified sales of the *Observer* and the *Sunday Times* may be interpreted as at least a minor indication of rising standards in public taste. On the other hand, it is too easy to make glib and facile assumptions about this undoubted improvement. For all that the *Observer* has increased its circulation, it still only sells just under 750,000 copies per week. The million-plus sales of the *Sunday Times* can be attributed partly to the recent innovation of a colour supplement. Bearing in mind that many households taking the *Observer* also take the *Sunday Times*, the proportion of the total population involved is absurdly small. In terms of daily papers, the General Council of the Press† has made a similar point: "It is significant that for every additional copy gained by the *Daily Telegraph* during the past year [1953] the tabloid newspapers added three." Furthermore, when it is claimed that a "quality" publication has increased its circulation by, say, 15 per cent in a year, this is again misleading because among the popular papers their sales are so large that it is simply not possible for them to make large percentage increases. T. R. Fyvel‡ makes the interesting suggestion that the increased popularity of the "quality" press has actually re-emphasized class distinctions, though it is doubtful whether, even if true, this is anything more than a marginal factor.

Compared with even the smallest daily or Sunday newspaper, the weekly and monthly "cultural" journals have an infinitesimally small

* Circulation 4,289,750 (April 1963).

† *The Press and the People*, First Annual Report of the General Council of the Press, 1954.

‡ Fyvel, T. R., *op. cit.*

circulation. Sales of periodicals in this category enjoyed a continuous increase immediately after the end of the war, then became steady or dropped slightly for a time, and finally began another upturn. In 1955 the *New Statesman*'s audited circulation was 70,598 copies;* the *Spectator* sold 38,353, and *Encounter* had a circulation in mid-1954 of about 15,000 copies. The *Listener* has more than doubled its sales since the war. As a generalization it might be asserted that the majority of these publications have benefited from the general wave of prosperity sweeping over the country as a whole. On the other hand these are, in almost all cases, very well-established publications (*Encounter* is an outstanding exception). New ventures in the same field have almost invariably failed—the market is so small that there is simply no room for extra competitors. Hoggart† concludes that "the present situation offers few grounds for satisfaction", for the swelling readership for these "quality" publications is merely marginal compared with the circulation of weeklies at the other end of the scale, with readerships (largely among young working-class women) of at least 500,000. These older magazines, like *Red Letter*, *Silver Star*, and *Oracle*, are supplemented by the new-style "pop" comics, like *Valentine*, *Roxy* and *Carissima*.

Book production in the United Kingdom is higher than in any other country. During 1963, for example, 20,367 titles were issued here, an increase of 7·9 per cent since 1962, compared with about 13,000 titles for the U.S.A., which has a population three times as large. Not all these titles referred to new books, of course: in fact, 14,711 came into this category.‡ About one-fifth of the total, both new issues and reprints, are works of fiction, and it is apparent that the major increase in book publishing has been in the field of technical and educational literature, in which paperbacks have played a great part. According to Cauter and Downham,§ it is probable that between 125 and 190 million separate volumes, including paperbacks, are sold in each year. In addition, there has been a very great

* In 1963 this had risen to over 87,000—by far the highest circulation of the political weeklies.

† Hoggart, R., *op. cit.*

‡ Figures from *The Bookseller*.

§ Cauter, T., and Downham, J. S., *op. cit.*

increase in the number of books issued from public libraries, especially during the last 25 years. During 1952–3, seven books were issued per head of the population compared with five in 1939. In Derby it appeared that those borrowing at least one book a week from the public library constituted about one in six from the working classes and people with elementary education, and one in four from the middle classes and people with secondary and/or further education. Again in Derby, one-third of those interviewed said they were currently reading a book. A 1950 Gallup Poll on the same subject gave a proportion of 55 per cent, higher than that found in, say, the U.S.A. or Sweden. When broken down into class divisions, it appeared in Derby that 40 per cent of the middle class and 26 per cent of the working class were reading a book at the time of the interview; those who had never read a book comprised 12 per cent and 23 per cent respectively.

So far, this discussion has confined itself to those leisure pursuits practised by majority groups within the population. A further example is ballroom dancing, which has elevated itself into becoming the second largest entertainment industry in the country (after the cinema). There are probably between 450 and 500 ballrooms used for that purpose alone, plus many more halls which cater for dancing, among other things. Attendances are estimated at 200 million a year, the majority being in the 17 to 25 age group. The money involved is about £25 million (a quarter of the amount at stake in cinema-going). Many dancers take an extremely serious interest in their hobby, and *The Economist** noted the "respectable" tone of most halls and the earnestness of the dancers' concentration.

Gambling, too, has become a nation-wide preoccupation. In the past, there has been an unconsciously organized attempt to categorize betting as an almost exclusively working-class phenomenon.†

* Most of the details in this paragraph derive from "Saturday Night at the Palais", *The Economist*, 14 February 1953.

† The argument runs as follows: the manual worker, confined to a dull job, constantly frustrated by his inability to make ends meet, reacts with dreams of sudden wealth and something for nothing. This is supplemented by the supposedly working-class ethos which discounts saving and encourages short-run hedonism.

Orwell* noted, during the Great Depression, how the incidence of betting, far from declining in the period of unemployment, actually increased:

> Even people on the verge of starvation can buy a few days' hope ("something to live for", as they call it) by having a penny on a sweep-stake. Organized gambling has now risen almost to the status of a major industry. Consider, for instance, a phenomenon like the football pools, with a turnover of about six million pounds a year, almost all of it from the pockets of working-class people.

Orwell, of course, was writing in 1936. Today, gambling *is* a major industry and the amount of money spent on football pools has risen beyond Orwell's wildest dreams, according to the statistics (Table 17) from the *Annual Report*† of the Churches' Council on Gambling. It estimates the total at £853 million but a reservation is implicit throughout the Report that it could be much higher: for example, a

TABLE 17

Form of gambling	1961 (£ million)	1962 (£ million)
Horses	440	540
Greyhounds	125	115
Football pools	101½	85½
Football (fixed odds)	50	60
Bingo	25	30
Premium Bonds	13½	15½
Fun fairs, etc.	7½	7½
Totals	762½	853½

clear opinion is expressed that the figure of £540 million given for betting on horses could be underestimated by as much as £100 million. "In a year when investment generally was thought to be slack, there was lavish investment in this direction, with high profits in most cases."

* Orwell, G., *The Road to Wigan Pier*, Gollancz, London, 1937.
† *Annual Report*, Churches' Council on Gambling, 1963.

Recent years have seen some interesting additions to the available opportunities for a flutter, and it is important to remember that football pools have proliferated enormously between 1936 and 1962 *despite* the competition of such new forms of gambling as bingo and premium bonds. Bingo entered this country from the U.S.A. some years ago but was already familiar to most households in the form of lotto, housey-housey or tombola. Its popularity was rapidly promoted by the frequency of wet afternoons in holiday camps, and although the first craze for bingo has perhaps been passed, it is unlikely that turnover is any lower than at the peak of 1961. The other major new attraction for gamblers is the Premium Bond, introduced by Mr. Harold Macmillan as Chancellor of the Exchequer in 1956, with these words*: "Let me say that this is not a pool or lottery, where you spend your money. The investor in the bond which I propose is saving his money. . . . But as long as he holds it saved, his reward, instead of interest, is the chance of winning a tax-free prize. . . . This is not gambling, for the subscriber cannot lose." The success of the Premium Bond scheme can be established by the fact that in June 1963 a total of 403 million bonds were held.

Following the 1960 Act, which made many forms of gambling legal, the whole pattern of gambling is changing. Legal betting shops have been established and have virtually abolished illegal street betting. The Churches' Council on Gambling suggests that, whatever the exact figure spent on horses, more than half went through the betting shops in 1962. "Some have considered that the betting-office turnover alone has reached £1000 million a year." Indeed, it might be surmised that the introduction of widespread off-course betting on horse-racing has attracted women and others who would not previously have indulged in surreptitious street-corner deals. Another development has been the Horse Race Betting Levy Board's charges on bookmakers to compensate for reduced attendances at courses and televised races, an arrangement which is still in its infancy.

As regards the people who actually patronize the *chemin de fer* and

* Quoted in Hughes, E., *Macmillan: Portrait of a Politician*, Allen & Unwin, London, 1962.

bingo clubs, betting shops and football pools, a recent Gallup Poll* showed that although 56 per cent of a nation-wide population sample approved of gambling and betting, not all carried their approval as far as practice. In fact, precisely the same proportion said they had not bet on a horse or a dog during the past twelve months, not even on special occasions like the Derby and the Grand National. The remaining 44 per cent who had bet could be distinguished as shown in Table 18. The pro-gamblers, regardless of class, are largely

TABLE 18

Frequency	%
Most days	2
Two or three times a week	4
Once a week	6
Once or twice a month	7
Less often	25
Total	44

men of middle age, and regional differences imply that there is less gambling in Scotland and the North than in the Midlands and the South.

Most people, whether approving of gambling or not, seemed prepared to discriminate between different sorts of betting, judging by their choice of particular games of chance they would like to see taxed. Casinos and other gambling clubs were singled out by the largest number as a proper subject of taxation, whereas only a minority wanted to tax fund-raising draws or lotteries. Even with the newest craze, bingo, half those interviewed were in favour of taxing it. The majority—58 per cent—were either indifferent or undecided about betting shops. Whether they have succeeded to the extent anticipated is another matter. When asked, "How do you usually place your bets nowadays?" 20 per cent claimed to use the betting shop, of whom 4 per cent only started betting since their opening.

* Francis, E. V., "The Way the Betting Goes", *Daily Telegraph*, 1 April 1963.

Some still patronized the street bookmaker or agent, others had an account with a bookmaker, and still others used the "amateur" bookie who runs a book as a sideline.

Only a very small proportion (2 per cent) actually bet on the course. As many as 86 per cent of those questioned for the Gallup Poll had not attended any kind of race meeting within the previous twelve months; only 9 per cent had gone to the race-course, and 4 per cent to the dog track. Faced with this kind of knowledge, it is doubtful whether the gamblers are as interested in the sport as in the gambling. The Churches' Council on Gambling, too, remarked that the "pools panel"* set up during the bad weather in 1963 confirmed their view that interest in pools and in football was "not identical". Their report adds: "It may well be that the 'pools panel' will have the effect of accentuating the decline in popularity of this form of betting."

The most obvious cause of the popularity of gambling is naturally the desire to make money. Yet, according to the Gallup Poll, less than one person in ten makes a profit on this betting: 24 per cent said they lost money, 18 per cent were just about even, and 9 per cent claimed to win. Half either did not know or did not bet at all. Among those who did know how much they lost on the pools and on betting of all kinds, 42 per cent had lost less than £10 and only 8 per cent had lost more than £20. Win or lose, however, most people were disinclined to take a sternly censorious view of gambling and betting on religious or moral grounds. In replying to the question: "Do you think the Church ought to protest strongly against betting or should they ignore it?" 67 per cent thought it should be ignored, 15 per cent had no view, and only 18 per cent wanted the Church to protest. Much the same result was obtained when people were interviewed on the desirability or otherwise of such habits as smoking and drinking.

Of the different forms of gambling, the football pools provide the

* For some weeks, whenever more than thirty matches were cancelled on any particular Saturday, the probable results were evaluated by a group of "experts" on the basis of the teams' past performance, etc. This much-criticized practice enabled the pools to continue operations when otherwise they would have been forced to close down temporarily.

greatest draw. Rather more than three out of five people said that either they personally (35 per cent) or other members of their family (26 per cent) had been staking money on them in the season 1962–3. Of the 35 per cent, one-fifth claimed to have filled in coupons every week. Bingo has been quick to acquire a substantial following, though it is still a minority pastime. Almost two people in five had played it at some time or other. Only 2 per cent played two or three occasions each week; 15 per cent confined their games to holidays and special occasions. Sweepstakes, draws and the like attract a smaller following: not quite one person in five takes part regularly. For this kind of gambling, Christmas and other occasions, or the possibility of supplementing the funds of some organization (generally political), provided the incentive for the majority.

Figures given in the *Report** of the Royal Commission on Betting, Lotteries and Gaming imply that, so far as the class factor is concerned, the percentage of men in the working classes who bet on the pools is higher than the percentage of those doing so in the other classes. While in terms of absolute numbers the working class may be predominant in gambling, however, an important proviso which must be noted here is the fact that the average amount of money wagered by each working-class individual may be very small. An insignificant number of upper-class people can bet with very large stakes at, say, Crockfords, thereby counteracting the economic contribution to gambling statistics made by the working class *en masse*.

Turning now to the vexed question of the hypothetical relationship between leisure, social status, and social class, it would perhaps be most appropriate to begin by outlining Thorstein Veblen's theory of the leisured classes.† In his book, published soon after World War I, he postulated that people are basically motivated, in everything they do, by the desire for status. Since status is not easily acquired, they generally pursue the acquisition of wealth as a compensatory mechanism. By emulating the expenditure patterns of the higher

* Royal Commission on Betting, Lotteries and Gaming: *Report* (Cmd. 8190), H.M.S.O., London, 1951.

† Veblen, T., *Theory of the Leisure Class*, London, 1924.

strata, they hope in turn to achieve the social position they so much value. Veblen argues that because material wealth is a passport to gaining social prestige, it eventually becomes intrinsically honourable. Since the desire for status is insatiable, so the lust for wealth becomes illimitable. One of the distinguishing features of the leisured class is its intrinsic freedom from the necessity to undertake paid employment. Leisure is desirable for its own sake and labour tends to be associated with social inferiority and hence to be regarded as degrading.* Veblen's theory is still relevant in contemporary society, although the view that conspicuous and ostentatious expenditure is alone sufficient for the acquisition of social prestige has been discarded. Other, more subtle criteria have been established as the membership qualifications for the social *élite*.

Controversy reigns over whether certain ways of spending leisure signify superior social status. If nothing else, the ability to sport a deep tan (acquired in Switzerland or Austria) on the 8.35 a.m. train to Waterloo, in January, is surely just as much a gesture of status as is voting Conservative or owning a Rolls-Royce. At the same time, it is apparent that the last hundred years has seen a considerable democratization of leisure. Hunting, shooting and fishing were originally the sole prerogative of the upper classes, and the discovery of the medicinal qualities present in sea-water initially benefited only the wealthier sections of the community. The evolution of the mass media has familiarized many people with upper-class methods of enjoying leisure, and these methods have consequently filtered through to a larger proportion of the population. Cheap transport has enabled everyone to recuperate at seaside resorts. The affluent society has encouraged the growth of even highly expensive leisure pursuits, such as yachting, motor-car racing and rallying, and holidays abroad.

When the idea of leisure is extended to include clubs and societies

* Veblen (*op. cit.*) made the interesting point that the manufacture of goods by manual labour is more expensive and wasteful than using machines; and so the hand-made product, despite its crudeness and imperfections, exudes an air of costliness which is a highly potent status symbol for the wealthy. For this reason, hand-carved and hand-painted pottery, and hand-blown glassware, are cherished possessions in the upper-class home.

of all kinds, then the implications of status are unavoidable. Clubs organized around the performance of certain prestige-conferring leisure activities, for instance, may deliberately engineer their membership regulations in order to preserve their exclusiveness. In Woodford, Willmott and Young* noted that although most clubs were not explicitly selective in their membership, there were exceptions: some controlled entry through the enforcement of high fees or more indirect means. "Supposing a plasterer or someone like that applied to join," one club member said. "We want something a little bit higher social standard than that." Compared with Bethnal Green, there were fewer meetings for a chat in the street, but more clubs and organizations. This could be said to reflect the more formal structure and middle-class atmosphere of Woodford itself. Older men typically belonged to the bowls or golf club, the Conservative or Rotary organizations. Women were members of the Women's Institute, the Townswomen's Guild or the tennis club. The survey concluded that 35 per cent of the middle-class population had attended at least one club in the month previous to the interview, compared with only 18 per cent of the working class. Bottomore's "Squirebridge"† apparently reflected the same pattern, for he writes that nearly all the town's voluntary organizations were characterized by strong influence towards segregation on lines of occupational (and hence social) status. In some cases, the tendency was obvious and even pardonable—in the trade and professional bodies, for example. Other factors were sometimes involved, however, such as the fixing of a high subscription or the establishment of a standard of behaviour unattainable (or seemingly so) for individuals of low occupational status. As Bottomore points out, the individual sees a club, society or association not only as a means of satisfying certain of his interests or needs, but also as a group of people with whom he may or may not feel that he can mix freely.

Bearing this last factor in mind, we can say that leisure may be a

* Young, M., and Willmott, P., *Family and Class in a London Suburb*, Routledge & Kegan Paul, London, 1960.

† Bottomore, T., "Social Stratification in Voluntary Organizations", in Glass, D. V. (ed.), *Social Mobility in Britain*, Routledge & Kegan Paul, London, 1954.

mark of status or, alternatively, a means of achieving status. Of the latter possibility, Bottomore argues that it is exceptional to find an individual seeking to climb the social scale by deliberately joining an organization whose members possess high occupational status. Upward mobility depends more on educational or occupational advancement, and membership of a particular voluntary group is more a confirmation of newly acquired status than a step towards acquiring that status. In general, the avenues towards higher social standing through leisure activities are narrow and limited. Trade union or political activity may bear fruit in this respect—the dustman can become Councillor Smith—or well-known figures in the field of, say, amateur sport can become what C. Wright Mills* calls "celebrities". Class may be significant in another way, however, inasmuch as an individual may be deterred from joining a leisure organization if, according to his own evaluation, the members of that organization belong largely to a different social stratum. In Squirebridge,† for example, the cricket club had a high proportion of Group A members (according to a threefold occupational classification) and the working class generally regarded it as rather "snobbish". This subjective appraisal undoubtedly intimidated many potential members in the lower occupational categories, even though, in some cases, this impression was erroneous. For instance, the Squirebridge cricket club drew half its present membership from the lower layers of the social structure.

In those organizations whose membership extended to all three occupational groups, official leadership was undoubtedly concentrated on the members with high social status. There is not necessarily anything sinister in this situation—the leaders may have been chosen because of various qualities of character or efficiency that were originally responsible for their high status. The large number of so-called vice-presidents in the local Conservative constituency association, for example, played only a negligible part in the party's affairs and must have been selected primarily for reasons of status. Distinctions of status used to be vitally important in the charitable

* Mills, C. Wright, *The Power Élite*, Oxford University Press, 1956.
† Bottomore, T., *op. cit.*

societies discussed by Rosalind Chambers,* where a clear dichotomy between the benefactors and the beneficiaries could be observed. Until comparatively recently, the leading individual in each Red Cross branch, Women's Institute or Women's Voluntary Service centre was almost invariably the most prominent woman in the upper classes. Even where the rules required some of the organizing members to be appointed by election, the results were usually a foregone conclusion. As a result of the war, the advent of the Welfare State, and the general processes of economic and social change, this position has altered. But the transition has been largely unnoticed by those working-class women who, according to Rosalind Chambers, often criticize women's organizations on the grounds that their members are superior, patronizing and condescending. Today, minor positions of authority are held in the Red Cross, W.I. and W.V.S. by women of all social levels. Participation in community service—largely a wartime development—has been continued and extended, although the lowest status groups are still in a minority. In most of the W.V.S. centres observed, for example, the vital condition of success seemed to be the presence of a key woman surrounded by a group of enthusiastic satellites. In some areas, this key woman was still in the upper-class category, but more often she was middle class (the wife of a business man or schoolmaster). At the lower levels, working-class women were given their chance to contribute, although some may be necessarily ruled out by such intangible factors as, say, their lack of a telephone, which in a rural area is almost indispensable. Rosalind Chambers concludes that faith in a divinely ordered, graded society is disappearing, since class consciousness is non-existent in many women. They join an organization to perform a specific function and are not worried by the different social origins of the other women in the group.†

* Chambers, R. C., "A Study of Voluntary Organizations", in Glass, D. V. (ed.), *Social Mobility in Britain*, Routledge & Kegan Paul, London, 1954.

† The situation is different in the U.S.A. In a study of Jews in Elmira, New York, it was found, for instance, that there was far more self-segregation of both Gentiles and Jews at the wife level than at the husband level. While 12 per cent of the Jewish men confined their social activities to purely Jewish organizations, 48 per cent of the wives did. In occupational terms, wives

A number of factors influence status differences within leisure organizations; the first of these, quoted by Bottomore,* is size. A small group functions as a whole, and its members are more likely to develop a common system of values, whereas, in the larger organizations, sub-groups emerge which almost always follow lines of occupational status. A clear instance of the latter concerned an informal social club in Squirebridge with 200 members, of whom 25 per cent were in group A, 25 per cent in group B and the remainder in Group C. There were no organized activities, and members attended merely to drink, talk, play billiards and darts. In practice, there was practically no contact between members of group C and the other two groups, and the club officials all belong to group A. Comparable examples may be quoted from the U.S.A. Lloyd Warner† found in Jonesville that "there is, in general, a sharp break between the upper middle and lower middle classes, with respect to the kind and amount of participation in associations. . . . There is little participation between the upper middle and lower middle classes." And Vance Packard‡ notes: "today, the two upper classes have substantially abandoned all associations, such as the lodges, that would bring them into contact with members of the three lower classes."

The other side of the coin emerges when examining the smaller groups centred around specific activities. In Squirebridge,§ one small hobbies club, with less than twenty members, emphasized the absence of occupational status distinctions within the organization, and suggested that interest and proficiency in the hobby were the only factors relevant to the achievement of high status. Their meetings were characterized by their informality, although the president was treated with some deference and was not addressed by his first

---

may be vital in securing high-level appointments for their husbands, and must therefore choose their social contacts carefully. See Dean, J. P., "Patterns of Socialization and Association Between Jews and Non-Jews", *Jewish Social Studies*, vii, 3 (1955).

* Bottomore, T., *op. cit.*

† Warner, W. Lloyd, *Democracy in Jonesville*, Harper, New York, 1959.

‡ Packard, V., *The Status Seekers*, Longmans, London, 1960.

§ Bottomore, T., *op. cit.*

name—no doubt because he was a company director, a J.P., and a founder of the club! Certainly, when the leisure activity requires skill, prestige may be gained by the possession of that skill. This may produce a status system differing from that produced by occupation. On the other hand, the two status systems may coincide (and therefore be indistinguishable) if the skills required within the club are similar to those required in a business or profession. For cultural and educational groups, to take an obvious example, membership is influenced by the individual's educational attainment, which is in turn closely correlated with occupational status. The Squirebridge branch of the Workers' Educational Association, therefore, had only one weekly wage-earner among its thirty members. As regards educational advancement, Cauter and Downham's Derby survey* showed that 59 per cent of the middle-class and 24 per cent of the working-class population had undertaken a part-time course of further education—usually an evening class—at some time or other. A partial explanation for this differential may be found in the reasons why people attend evening classes. The type of course chosen usually depends on the job, and people apparently enrol in the hope of promotion within their present occupation, not in order to change their form of employment. Hence evening classes are not particularly helpful to those in manual work.

Bottomore's second factor† influencing status distinctions within the voluntary groups of Squirebridge was the nature of the organization's activities. Among those clubs and societies having no specific function, there is no common interest to unite the members. This being so, there is a tendency for small groups to form, consisting of members who have something in common—usually occupation—outside the club. By contrast, social differentiation in organizations exercising specific activities is based, according to Bottomore, on the type of activity. This is especially obvious in the case of charitable organizations which include, as members, both the dispensers and recipients of charity, and for service and ex-service organizations, where status distinctions are based on the "officer" and "other ranks"

* Cauter, T., and Downham, J. S., *op. cit.*
† Bottomore, T., *op. cit.*

criterion. Since the ex-officers are usually those with higher occupational status in civilian life, however, the membership in such societies usually follows the conventional pattern.

One aspect of Veblen's theory still holds good, namely, the fundamental importance of money in gaining entry to certain socially desirable forms of leisure. Among clubs hoping to maintain their exclusive membership, high subscriptions help to eliminate the lower income groups. Even when an individual has gained access to the organization of his choice, finance again assumes great significance, especially where the organization indulges in a variety of optional activities. Prestige is acquired by those who participate most fully, and this depends largely on having sufficient time and money. Frequency of meetings is also important in accentuating or weakening status distinctions: the Rotary Club may hold a weekly lunch, while the horticultural society may only meet once a year at the annual show. Bottomore* argues that members are more likely to enjoy a kind of "rough equality" if their organization meets frequently. Where meetings occur at rare intervals, there is no opportunity to break down social barriers.

Finally, it must be borne in mind that not all leisure pursuits are in any way correlated with occupational (or any other form of) status. Nearly half the population are cinema-goers, for instance, but the difference in attendance rates for the working class and middle class is not significant. Cauter and Downham† reveal that, in Derby, 49 per cent of the former and 40 per cent of the latter go to the cinema frequently (i.e. more than once a month). As we have already seen, the class connotations of television-set ownership are fast disappearing (although as to what programmes are watched in different households, this is a separate question). Even with hobbies of all kinds, it appeared in Derby that 46 per cent of the working class had no hobbies, compared with 31 per cent of the middle class. On the other hand, those working-class members who did have hobbies typically undertook more (at least two) than their middle-class counterparts.

* Bottomore, T., *op. cit.*
† Cauter, T., and Downham, J. S., *op. cit.*

CHAPTER 6

Political Aspects of Society

Party is organized opinion.
(DISRAELI.)

Political constitutions are made not from wood and stone but from the dispositions of their citizens, which turn the scale and draw everything in their wake.
(PLATO.)

The modern proletariat ends by believing that by flocking to the polls its direct participation in power will be ensured.
(MAX WEBER.)

POLITICAL PARTIES

Like all other large-scale organizations, the political party is bureaucratic in form. A strong hierarchy of centralized administration is built up, and power tends to be concentrated in the hands of a few top officials. Once the position of these leaders has been consolidated, they become established and irremovable, creating a kind of oligarchical rule which Weber believed to be inevitable: "The formation of oligarchies within the various forms of democracy is the outcome of organic necessity which consequently affects every organization, the socialists or even anarchists." Why is a party organization necessary? The essential functions of a party bureaucracy are to maintain and improve party efficiency in order to secure the votes necessary to place the party in power, and also to provide the machinery essential for the two-way communication of ideas between the party leadership and the party rank-and-file. In short, electoral success depends almost entirely on the efforts of the party organization.

A political party itself is a formal union of individuals and affiliated groups, having similar views on leading political questions. The party deliberately tries to gain power so that it may put these views into practice. The party system has considerable disadvantages. Once in power, the party is difficult to control, and the leadership may not always be responsive to the wishes of party members. On the other hand, government without parties is virtually impossible to envisage, since Parliament would then be little more than a debating club. Moreover, a clear dichotomy between two parties, while it may lead to misrepresentation of their real attitudes and policies, does stimulate public interest in politics. This country favours the two-party system, which does not mean that only two parties exist, but that only two parties are capable of forming a government. Each party encompasses a wide range of opinion, and although this arrangement does increase the difficulty of identifying a party's particular "brand image" clearly, it does have the signal merit that it removes the necessity for splinter parties or groups. Indeed, the chief advantage of the two-party system lies in the fact that it almost inevitably produces a government with an effective majority over all other groups combined.

The British political scene is simply portrayed in the following diagram whereby the main groups—Conservatives, Socialists,

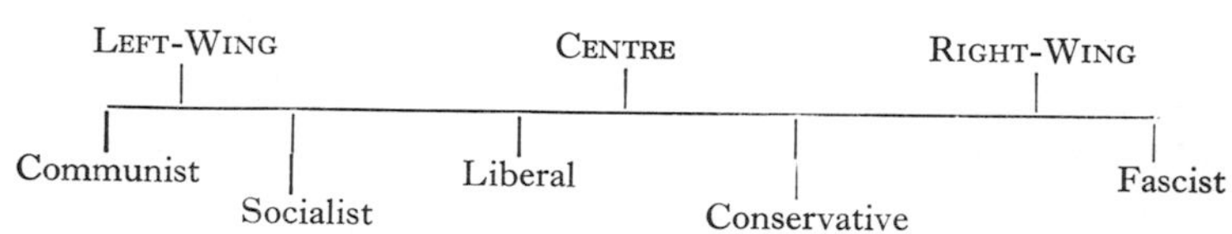

Liberals, Communists and Fascists—are arranged along a continuum from left to right. To some people, this classification is unconvincing because, it is argued, the Communists and Fascists have something in common which sets them apart from the democratic parties. To avoid this criticism, the ends of the continuum could be pulled round to form a circle, with the Communists and Fascists being placed at the same point on the circumference. However, the end result is the same—the essential point is that each party contains an amalgam of interests. One of the most unenviable tasks of any party leader is to maintain a sufficient degree of unity and coherence within his party, and to justify the allegiance of individuals at the two extremes of the organization.

The Communist Party was one of the by-products of the Russian Revolution of 1917. It operates a newspaper, the *Daily Worker*, which suffers permanent financial difficulties owing to its lack of advertising revenue.* The circulation of this paper is approximately 30,000 copies daily, a figure which reflects the membership of the party as a whole† although an indeterminate number of people belong to the category of "fellow-travellers", that is, they support the Communist policy but do not carry party membership cards. Because the appeal of Marxism lies mainly with the proletariat, it is not surprising that the Communist Party derives most of its support from the working class, to whom are added a proportion of intellectuals. The numerical significance of the latter dropped sharply following Khrushchev's Twentieth Congress speech denouncing Stalin and the 1956 Hungarian Revolution.‡ Despite the fact that two Communist M.P.s were elected to Parliament in 1945, the party is not represented there at present, and its main source of strength is the trade unions.§

There is no single Fascist group, but possibly the most long-lived is the Union Movement, which was regarded seriously for a short time in the 1930's.

In addition, there are two other Fascist groups, the British

* This problem is due partly to the Communists' ideological views on advertising, and partly to the unwillingness of potential advertisers (including the Government) to be associated with a Communist newspaper. The *Daily Worker*'s advertising revenue in one year is less than the *Daily Express* can earn in one day.

† In March 1963 the chairman of the organization committee, Mr. W. Lauchlan, said that the C.P.G.B. had 34,372 members plus 4666 Young Communists.

‡ See Wood, N., *Communism and British Intellectuals*, Gollancz, London, 1959.

§ For further information on Communism in Britain, see Carew Hunt, R. N., *The Theory and Practice of Communism*, Geoffrey Bles, London, 1950.

National Party and the National Socialists. The latter is the most bigoted of the three. It stands for the expulsion of the Jews, the abolition of democracy, and the establishment in Britain of a Racial Nationalist Folk-state. Its members would wear uniform in public but for the 1937 Public Order Act, which itself was passed as a result of Fascist "black-shirt" and Communist "brown-shirt" clashes in the East End of London. The National Socialist movement opposes democracy so fiercely that it does not even fight elections, whereas the British National Party does make some attempt to have its voice heard through the channels of democracy.* The B.N.P. does not support the wearing of uniforms and adulation of Hitler's memory. Its policy is that West Indians should be sent home at British expense and that a political climate should be created in Britain such that Jews and other non-European aliens would prefer to go elsewhere.†

The old-established political parties—the Liberals and the Conservatives—date from that period in the nineteenth century when universal adult suffrage, at least for all males, was beginning to become a tangible prospect. Particularly after the 1867 Reform Act, the need for central party organizations became acute. A Liberal Party headquarters was established, modelled on the extremely successful Birmingham group of Liberals, and the Conservatives set up their National Union of Conservative and Unionist Associations. Earlier remarks about the bureaucratic nature of political party organizations may be aptly illustrated by Diagram 1 of the distribution of power within the Conservative movement.

It is no part of the purpose of this book to analyse party organizations in detail; suffice to say that, as the diagram suggests, the party leader is the king-pin in this elaborate structure of committees, conferences and M.P.s. Once appointed, he is only removed with difficulty; he exercises direct control over the party's propaganda

* The B.N.P. fought a very small number of seats in Deptford and Islington in the local government elections of May 1962; the best it could do was 9·75 per cent of the poll in one ward in Deptford. The Union Movement contested sixty-odd seats at the same elections, claiming an average vote of 5·5 per cent.

† For further information, see Cross, C., *The Fascists in Britain*, Barrie & Rockliff, London, 1961.

DIAGRAM 1

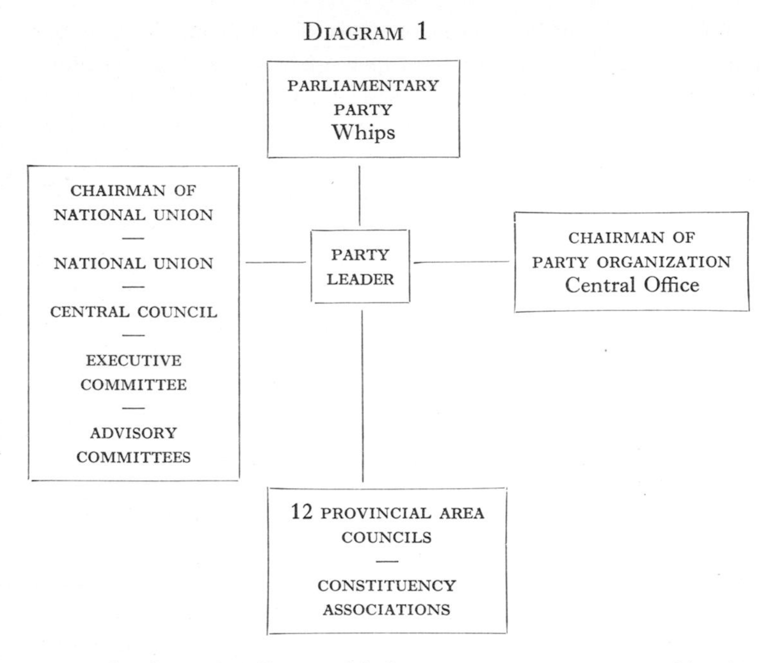

organ, the Central Office, and is in a position to exert considerable influence over the National Union. His own threats of resignation can be the ultimate sanction in maintaining his personal authority over the Parliamentary Party and the party as a whole. It is interesting and revealing to note that, in the Conservative Party, the leader does not even attend the Annual Conference. Its resolutions, if approved, may be communicated to him *but are not binding*. The function of the Annual Conference, in this as in other political groups, is not to establish policy but rather to act as a morale-building session for the loyal party workers.

The Labour Party is currently the second component of the British two-party system. Although the party was not formed officially until 1906, the first working-class M.P. to enter Parliament was in fact Keir Hardie almost 20 years previously. The closing years of the nineteenth century had seen increasing pressure from the Trades Union Congress, and other quarters, for the creation of a new party to fulfil specifically working-class needs. The Labour Party had an immediate success, gaining over fifty seats in the 1906 elections, becoming the Opposition and forming a minority government by 1924.* It replaced the Liberals, who had reached their apogee in the years just prior to World War I, and who have since declined almost as rapidly as the Labour Party has ascended. The organization of the Labour Party is equally as bureaucratic as that of the Conservative movement, being based on a federation of the constituency parties, the trade unions, the Co-operative Societies and certain socialist societies. Each of these is represented at the Annual Conference at the rate of one delegate for every 5000 members, an arrangement which leaves the trade unions as by far the most dominant group within the party. The Annual Conference, however, provides an opportunity for genuine debate, although the views of the National Executive generally prevail. It is at the Annual Conference that the twenty-five members of this executive, the party's controlling administrative body, are elected. The party leader and his deputy are *ex officio* members of the National Executive and are elected, not by the conference, but by the Parliamentary Party alone. Theoretically, the party leader is subject to annual re-election. However, such is the vital importance of his position and the electoral value of his personality, that he stands very little chance of being deposed; and, in fact, this has never happened.

Whether the Liberals are on the verge of a revival is more difficult to ascertain at the time of writing: in 1959 they gained second place in twenty-six constituencies, and ran Labour a close third in many others. Labour suffered its third successive electoral defeat in that year, and the Conservatives have won with increasing majorities in all three elections since 1951, an unprecedented feat in this century. On the other hand, the Liberals still have negligible representation in Parliament—and, in politics, no prizes are awarded to those who come second.† In 1964, the Liberals collected over three million

* On the other hand, the party has only once governed with an electoral majority, from 1945 to 1951.

† See Abrams, M., "Who Are the New Liberals?", the *Observer*, 1 July 1962, for an attempt to analyse the sources of Liberal support.

votes and nine seats in the House of Commons, but, as before, it would be rash to assume that this marks a permanent resurgence.

POLITICAL ATTITUDES

Before making any attempt to trace any connection between voting behaviour and other sociological considerations, it would be as well to make the initial proviso that the science of psephology is only about half a century old. As D. E. Butler* remarks, "A very great deal more work must be done before any satisfactory or comprehensive general theory emerges about the reasons why people hold particular political beliefs." On the other hand, "ideas about the activity of pressure groups, the structure of parties, and the nature of elections, are radically different from those of a generation ago, simply because of the hard labour of scholars who have sought to describe and explain them". Clearly psephology has achieved something, although it is a little disappointing to be told, after all the elaborate and expensive sampling, the compilation and analysis of statistics, that "class is the social attribute most clearly correlated with party allegiance."

Even before the connection between voting behaviour and class was objectively established, many writers had tried to show some correlation between the two. Tonnies, for example, suggested that political affiliations are conditioned by a combination of economic factors and class/status consciousness. This may have been true in the context of Germany in the 1920's, when many of the poorer classes sycophantically voted to please their economic masters and social superiors. Tonnies questions the Marxian view that economic conflicts cannot take place within a single class—for example, striking electricians do not always consider the factory closures which their strike action may provoke. At the same time, he does not rule out economic and political conflicts based on class divisions—e.g. struggles between workers and employers—even if this kind of conflict is not necessarily the typical pattern. It has certainly not been the prevailing experience of the U.S.A.

* Butler, D. E., *The Study of Political Behaviour*, Hutchinson, London, 1958.

The traditional and commonplace notion of the connection between voting behaviour and class is that the Labour Party will be supported by the working class and the Conservatives by the middle classes. This sort of generalization presupposes that many political conflicts are based on disputes between the social classes. According to Eysenck,* whichever way the "national cake" is cut, "some people will receive more than others and the interests of one group will almost infallibly be opposed to the interests of another group". It is out of such situations that political parties emerge, based primarily on the differences of occupational and economic status that are an inevitable concomitant of any economically competitive society. For the purposes of this discussion, the status classifications used by the Gallup Poll are of value because the British Institute of Public Opinion has carried out a study of the relationship between social status and political attitude, involving a national sample of about 9000 people.† The B.I.P.O. listed the following status groups:

Group A: "Well-to-do men (or their wives) working in the higher professions, e.g. wealthier chartered accountants, lawyers, clergymen, doctors, professors, or in higher ranks in business."

Group B: "Professional workers not in the top category. Salaried clerical workers such as bank clerks; qualified teachers; owners and managers of large shops; supervisory grades in factories who are not manual workers; farmers."

Group C: "By far the biggest group. Manual workers, shop assistants, cinema attendants, clerks, agents."

Group D: "Very poor: people without regular jobs or unskilled labourers or living solely on Old Age Pension. Housing will be poor. They can only afford necessities."

These status groups each felt a subjective awareness of their membership in class categories, and, by and large, there was a considerable measure of agreement regarding to which class each

* Eysenck, H. J., *Sense and Nonsense in Psychology*, Penguin Books, 1957.
† Quoted in Eysenck, H. J., *op. cit.*

status group belonged. Most of Group A (57 per cent) tended to think of themselves as upper and upper middle class; most of Group B (58 per cent) as middle class. Fifty-five per cent and 76 per cent of Groups C and D respectively felt themselves to be working class. Of course, this still leaves a significant margin of deviants, but for the moment these will be ignored.

What, in fact, was the relationship between social status and political attitudes? The figures given in Table 19 support the kind

TABLE 19

Status group	Conservative (%)	Labour (%)	Liberal (%)	Other (%)	Don't know (%)	Total number
A	77	8	11	—	3	447
B	63	16	12	1	10	1855
C	32	47	9	1	11	4988
D	20	52	9	1	18	1621
Totals	3411	3545	894	60	1001	8911

of conclusion one would have reached on *a priori* evidence, namely, that the upper, upper middle and middle classes tend to vote Conservative, while the remainder tend to vote Labour.

So far, we have assumed that voting behaviour is always precisely and logically planned, and that the voter's primary concern will be to translate the objective criteria of his existence into relevant political terms. But even if, under normal circumstances, the working class would be better off under a Labour Government, prevailing world conditions may produce a situation where the working class would in fact be relatively worse off (than under preceding Conservative rule). This being so, one is not surprised to find the normal correlation between class and political attitudes to be a trifle confused, since some members of the working class may intermittently believe that the Conservative party represents their interests more closely than Labour.

In turning now to consider those deviants who, although belonging objectively to certain status groups according to occupational criteria, persist in regarding themselves subjectively as members of other classes, the primary consideration to bear in mind is the unquestioned tendency of an increasing proportion of the working classes (in occupational terms) to consider themselves as middle class. According to D. E. Butler and Richard Rose,* "the swing to the Conservatives [culminating in their 1959 election victory] cannot be dismissed as an ephemeral veering of the electoral breeze". It could be traced ultimately to the chief social change of the 1950's, namely, "the gradual erosion of traditional working class attitudes". This development may be ascribed to a combination of the following causes:

(1) A steady decline in the number of manual wage-earners.
(2) A rapid rise in living standards for all sections of the community, but most pronounced for the lower income groups; ownership of cars and consumer durables is now a far more widespread phenomenon.
(3) The decline of the traditionally class-conscious, older working-class groups.
(4) Housing migration from urban slum-areas into new suburban estates.
(5) Increase in home ownership, an effect tending to diminish the impact of the traditional Marxist dichotomy between owners and non-owners.
(6) The culturally "classless" influence of the mass media, particularly TV and the women's magazines.
(7) The growing tendency for leisure activities to centre around the home and family rather than the trade union branch, the chapel or the local Co-op.

These changes are together tending to weaken the old, proletarian class-consciousness of at least the younger and more prosperous workers, although the trend is as yet proceeding slowly and almost surreptitiously. One basic certainty is that the working class is

* Butler, D. E., and Rose, R., *The British General Election of 1959*, Macmillan, London, 1960.

steadily shrinking in size, even as judged by the objective tests of income and occupation, but more rapidly if judged by the subjective tests of social attitudes and aspirations. C. A. R. Crosland* goes further to suggest that the decline of the working class is actually an inevitable process with no foreseeable end:

> The rise in manufacturing productivity, which permits greater output to be achieved with a smaller industrial work-force; the continued relative growth of the distributive and service trades; the spread of automation; the increase within large firms of research, merchandizing, sales and office staff relative to the manual labour force—all these changes imply a continuing move away from a proletariat towards a salariat. In the United States, white-collar workers now exceed blue-collar workers in numbers; and Britain is moving in the same direction—as, indeed, are all advanced industrial countries.

Against this background most electors in 1959 found the outlook of the Conservatives "more in tune with the times than that of Labour, which often seemed rooted in the past".† Labour was often associated—whether correctly or not is irrelevant—with old issues, like nationalization and old people (the party's biggest propaganda effect in 1959 concerned old age pensions). Old candidates played their part, too, in damaging Labour's fortunes, since the average Labour candidate was 5 years older than his Conservative counterpart.

Hitherto, the chief cause of Labour's difficulties has been no more than mentioned, but Dr. Mark Abrams‡ has examined the problem more minutely in his recent study. Dr. Abrams observes that the basic and essentially simple situation is that the Labour Party is very largely identified with the interests of a class to which many of its supporters no longer consider themselves to belong. In his survey, something like a third of the party's working-class supporters (classified by income and occupation) placed themselves outside the working class entirely. Nearly a fifth of the labouring working class (the lowest occupational classification used by Dr. Abrams) placed themselves in the "skilled working-class" category. The very act of

* Crosland, C. A. R., *Can Labour Win?*, Fabian Society, 1960.

† Butler, D. E., and Rose, R., *op. cit.*

‡ Abrams, M., "Why Labour Has Lost Elections", three-part study in *Socialist Commentary*, 1960.

voting non-Labour may well be one way in which the individual demonstrates to himself that he is not, or not any longer, a member of the working class. In another study, of Liberal voters, Dr. Abrams* found that two-thirds described themselves as middle class (about 10 per cent refused to classify themselves at all, usually on the grounds that they did not believe in the class system). When asked why they thought themselves to be middle class, many Liberals pointed to their occupations (e.g. "Because I learned my trade—brewery technician—at an L.C.C. training college"), whereas most Labour and Conservative voters justified their class claims on grounds either of income or of family background.

Bonham's analysis† of the motivations behind voting behaviour is interesting because he tried to unravel the various components of the class situation and estimate their relative effects on political attitudes. The first such component he takes is income, which he correlates with Conservative and Labour votes: as income falls, so the Conservative vote declines, and vice versa. D. E. Butler's short survey of *The Floating Voter*‡ substantiates this broad generalization. Incidentally, Butler shows that the Liberals come nearest to attracting support from all classes and income groups. In his table (Table 20) which strikingly reveals the changes in political opinion since publication of the B.I.P.O. analysis (see p. 164), the figures are expressed

TABLE 20

Occupational and income category	Conservative	Labour	Liberal	Total
Professional and managerial	69	6	25	100
Other non-manual workers	48	22	30	100
Skilled workers	20	60	20	100
Unskilled workers	22	61	17	100
Totals	31	47	22	100

* Abrams, M., "Who Are the New Liberals?", the *Observer*, 1 July 1962.
† Bonham, J., *The Middle Class Vote*, Faber, London, 1954.
‡ Butler, D. E., "The Floating Voter", the *Sunday Times*, 17 March 1963.

as percentages of a nationwide sample of electors who had expressed definite party preferences. House and car ownership were also correlated with party preference in the expected pattern.

The second class component examined by Bonham was the classical Marxian dichotomy: the distinction between employers and employees, or, in Marxian terms, between *bourgeoisie* and proletariat. Among business proprietors, the Conservative vote tends to be maintained whatever the income. In Butler's survey,* a Northampton plumber said, "Perhaps I vote Conservative because I'm self-employed", and a Newcastle publican's wife said, "We used to vote Labour, but we look at things differently now that we have our own business." Among employees, the Labour vote tends to rise sharply as income falls. Bonham's third class component† was the contrast between manual and non-manual occupations. Here it is characteristically found that, even in the lower income groups, non-manual employees largely vote Conservative, while manual workers typically support Labour. However, as we have already seen, a general shift from manual to non-manual occupations in society, coupled with an overall rise in standards of living, may favour the Conservatives. Bonham concluded that proprietorship seems to be the most important factor influencing the Conservative vote; the others, such as industrial status, intellectual status and economic status, are merely reinforcing elements.

The final topic, in this section, must concern the social composition of the party organizations. A study of Greenwich revealed that the officials in both the main party organizations came from higher status categories than the party rank and file, supporters and voters. Homogeneity in the Labour Party was greater than among the Conservatives. To put it another way, the Conservatives represented a wider cross-section of the community than the Labour Party, which was heavily overweighted by manual workers. The other source of information on this question is Bottomore's article on "Squirebridge".‡ It was found, in a comparison between the two main

* Butler, D. E., *op. cit.* † Bonham, J., *op. cit.*

‡ Bottomore, T., "Social Stratification in Voluntary Organizations", in Glass, D. V. (ed.), *Social Mobility in Britain*, Routledge & Kegan Paul, London, 1954.

political groups, that the Conservatives had a higher proportion of women members, a higher average age level, and a larger number of members from the top occupational categories. Of the sixteen Conservative Party local officials, twelve were from Group A, four from Group B and none from Group C (in a threefold classificatory system), although 40 per cent of the party's membership came from the latter group. Membership of Conservative organizations was apparently regarded as a means of achieving prestige, whereas Labour organizations, on the other hand, did not carry prestige and often aroused active disapproval. Of the eighteen members in the local constituency leadership, one was from Group A, one from Group B, and sixteen from Group C. In general, active party workers seem to be no more than a small minority of the party's supporters, probably those with more leisure at their disposal than the majority.

TRADE UNIONS

The political importance of the trade unions stems not only from their close relationship to the Labour Party, but also from their force as a militant pressure group exercising influence through the Trades Union Congress and the individual union headquarters. Over seventy trade unions are directly affiliated to the Labour Party, and they exert a very great power over the party's Annual Conference by means of the "block vote" system. At the 1960 conference, for example, the trade unions commanded a vote of 5½ million out of a total 6½ million. Trade unions may sponsor candidates for Parliament, and owing to their strength they are able to place their nominees in safe constituencies, so that, if Labour loses an election, it is generally the non-union candidates who are defeated. In the 1951 General Election, for example, thirty-five out of the thirty-six candidates sponsored by the National Union of Mineworkers were elected, despite the fact that the Conservatives were returned to power in Parliament as a whole. The Parliamentary Labour Party's attitude to the unions is somewhat ambivalent. On the one hand they feel that, as in 1959, the party may suffer through the unpopularity of the unions, an unpopularity fostered by injudiciously timed official strikes, and minor unofficial strikes. On the other hand, the party is aware that its main source of revenue is the unions, which impose a "political levy" on the majority of their members.

About 180 unions are affiliated to the T.U.C. In 1959 these unions had a total membership of 8,128,000, in addition to which there were about 222,000 trade unionists whose unions were not affiliated to the T.U.C. This overall figure—of 8,350,000—represents a decline of nearly 250,000 since 1957, yet in the same period the numbers of people at work in British industry increased by about 170,000—from 23,130,000 to 23,300,000. As Michael Shanks* remarks: "The proportion of all workers willing to join trade unions is therefore declining, and so far as one can see this process looks like continuing." One of the main reasons for this trend is the general decline in the importance of manual workers, and a steady growth in the numbers of white-collar and professional workers, who are cautious about forming themselves into unions. Even if they do, they are unlikely to associate themselves with the politically left-wing T.U.C. The other basic cause is the decline of a number of primary industries which are traditionally heavily unionized—notable examples include ship-building, coal-mining and the railways.

The British trade union system is dominated by the craft unions, primarily because the system developed "in the days when the only groups of workers with the organizational skill, the financial resources, the cohesion and solidarity to build up unions and withstand the assaults of the employers were the craftsmen".† As a result, the T.U.C. is chiefly comprised of an extraordinary variety of tiny craft unions—such as, for example, the National Union of Basket, Cane, Wicker, and Fibre Furniture Makers of Great Britain and Ireland (126 members), and the Wool Shear Workers' Trade Union of Sheffield (64 members). These craft unions—each possessing its own jealously guarded traditions and privileges—may be contrasted with the two great "general workers' unions", the Transport

* Shanks, M., *The Stagnant Society*, Penguin Books, 1961. I am greatly indebted to this book for much of the material used in this section.

† Shanks, M., *op. cit.*

and General Workers' Union (T.G.W.U.), and the General and Municipal Workers (N.U.G.M.W.), which represent unskilled employees in a vast range of different industries.

Each union, whatever its size, tends to be bureaucratically organized—this is inevitable in the larger unions—with a central headquarters for the national officials, a hierarchy of area, district and branch offices down to the rank-and-file members. Each of these levels has its own particular problem. Union leaders, for instance, are normally only chosen from the rank-and-file, usually from among individuals who failed to reach their educational ceiling at school. Social changes since 1944 are bound to create problems for the unions in the long run, since there is now less likelihood that talented youths will be content to remain in manual work.* Union leaders are either appointed or elected, but either way they are seldom removed from office, a fact which recalls Weber's remarks about the difficulty of removing bureaucratic officials. Apart from the increasing disinclination of young people to leave school at 15 and take up manual work, the economic rewards of becoming a union leader are manifestly not great. Very few general secretaries draw more than £2000 a year, and the president of the Amalgamated Engineering Union, with nearly a million members under his control, is paid a salary of £1300 a year plus £100 London allowance.†

Another problem faced by the unions is the generally weak nature of communications between the leadership and the membership. This can be attributed to a combination of the unions' hierarchical structure, a diffused chain of command, and situational factors unavoidably producing different attitudes at the various levels within the union (the leaders have to consider strategy and diplomacy, while the members merely know that their wives are complaining because

* The same problem exists in the Civil Service. "A career from the bottom of the Service to the top is now feasible for the able entrant: but the stream of able entrants at the bottom is likely to dry up." See Mackenzie, W. J. M., and Grove, J. W., *Central Administration in Britain*, Longmans, London, 1957.

† Among the newer white-collar unions in Britain, too, general secretaries may draw quite reasonable salaries—in one or two cases amounting to £4000 per year.

the wage packet won't go round). Because the General Secretary's income is pegged, the salaries of other officials lower down the ladder must also be pegged if the differentials are not to be upset. Average salaries thus range from £750 to £1250. Nearly every union is seriously under-staffed: this must be the case if, as in the case of the railwaymen, there was in 1952 only one official to every 12,000 workers.* Against this background, it is not surprising that communications are weak between head office and the ordinary member. This weakness only enhances the underlying suspicion felt by the rank-and-file, who fear that

> once he has been exposed to influences from outside his class, the Trade Union official will desert and join the "bosses". . . . The Unions try to guard against this in two ways. . . . One way is to try to keep the centre as weak as possible, so that power is diffused among the active members. The other is to try to keep the leaders chained to a proletarian way of life, by keeping their salaries too low for anything else.†

With the coming of full employment, and the adoption of more moderate policies by the unions since 1926, the average member has stopped taking any active interest in his union's affairs. Most unions have a very low series of attendance figures at branch meetings. It is not uncommon for no more than about 10 or 15 per cent of the members to cast their votes in elections for even the most important posts—the presidency or general secretaryship. Indeed, the actual proportion of votes may be much lower than this, although the printers' unions constitute an important exception: their organization is based on "chapels" at each factory, with compulsory attendance and fines levied on absentees. Moreover, meetings are held immediately after working hours, rather than in the evening.

This pervading apathy has the effect of making the unions appear much more left-wing than they actually are. For the most part, the only active participants in union affairs are the 150,000 shop stewards. The unattractiveness of this job stems primarily from the fact that it

* According to Michael Shanks (*op. cit.*), there are at present about 3000 full-time officials to cater for some 8,350,000 unionists, i.e. one official to every 2780 members.

† Shanks, M., *op. cit.*

involves a good deal of hard work for little or no reward. The shop steward may even be losing money, because he sacrifices the chance to gain promotion or overtime. By acting as the spokesman for the workers he runs the risk of being classed as a trouble-maker by his employer and of being dismissed (though most unions will fight very hard against victimization of this kind). Hence there is very little competition for shop stewards' posts, and any organized pressure group can easily exercise a disproportionate power within the union by having its nominees appointed or elected to fill these vital positions in the union hierarchy. The best example of this—though by no means the only one—is of course the Communist Party, which, with a total union membership of not much more than 20,000, was able to control the 233,000-strong Electrical Trade Union and to wield considerable power in a number of others, including the Amalgamated Engineering Union and the National Union of Mineworkers.

The manifest functions of trade unions have changed since they were first formed, since much of the exploitation which originally inspired the union movement has been removed. Nevertheless, the unions will always be concerned with certain basic considerations, such as the maintenance of their members' standard of living. The 1944 T.U.C. Annual Report added two other aims, namely, the preservation of full employment, and the extensions of the influence of workpeople over the policies and purposes of industry. The unions' function as friendly societies has also been important—it is, in a way, an extension of their general protective duties. Apart from these permanent and continuing tasks, the unions have periodically sponsored other policies: after World War I, for example, syndicalism and other political ideas were prevalent, but have since been replaced by more moderate aims based on Fabian gradualism.

The bitter and implacably hostile relationships between the trade unions and the employers 50 years ago have now been softened, although the unions are still burdened by a long collective memory of unemployment, dismissals, redundancies, low wages, etc. Periodic downturns in business prosperity help to revive the spectre of the Great Depression and to keep these memories alive, but the wartime co-operation fostered by Bevin as Minister of Labour has borne permanent fruit to some degree. The Government now consults the T.U.C. on issues likely to affect labour, and institutionalized machinery exists for conciliation and negotiation in industrial disputes.

In this section we have touched upon some, though not all, of the contemporary issues facing the trade unions. Michael Shanks concludes that most of the defects in the movement could be put right by spending some more money, which would mean raising ordinary subscriptions fairly substantially. On the other hand, this would do no harm, since unionists at present are not financing their unions adequately. In 1912, dues in the Amalgamated Society of Engineers (forerunner of the present A.E.U.) amounted to 1*s*. 9*d*. a week, with the average wage rate in Manchester at 38*s*. a week. In 1959 the basic craftsman's wage in engineering was £9 6*s*. 8*d*. a week, while average actual earnings for men during that year came to nearly £14 a week; union dues were 2*s*. 3*d*. a week. In other words, they had fallen from over 4 per cent of the basic weekly wage to less than 1 per cent.* If the quality of trade union officials could be improved, the unions might make more progress in improving their members' conditions outside the narrow field of wages, and their impact on economic and social policy might be greater.

* This example is taken from Cyriax, G., and Oakeshott, R., *The Bargainers*.

CHAPTER 7

Social Controls: Religion

How these Christians love one another.

(TERTULLIAN.)

That Friday to the following Easter Monday—a time when the young English could relax. Except that I noticed something else. As the evening drew near, that is also to say at the very time when Christ was descending ever lower into the depths of Hell, so all decency seemed to vanish among these young people. Alcohol played its part and by the time darkness had fallen, the Bentleys and Rolls-Royces had begun to pour into the quarter. I stepped over the pools of vomit.

(JEAN GENET.)

RELIGION IN CONTEMPORARY BRITAIN

Any answer to the question of what sort of impact religion is making on the lives of people today must unavoidably be in terms of a decreasing and (in some cases) almost negligible influence. This may be attributable to a combination of many factors, including disillusionment with older systems of belief, the cynicism generated by two World Wars, and the power of scientific and rationalist thought. Some people argue that even if religion as such is not important in our society, religious *values* are deeply ingrained in our culture and in that of the U.S.A. However, it is a debatable question as to whether moral values are ever generated, or are merely underwritten, by religion. If the latter is true, then the dominant values operative in our society cannot be accurately described as religious at all. The attenuated role of religion can probably be described most satisfactorily, however, by recalling that a religion is supposed to provide a general theory of the universe: it explains, provides a means of control, and enables predictions to be made. In modern industrial society, scientific theories have eroded most of the religious explanations of life, and science certainly provides more efficient methods of control and prediction. Yet it would be a mistake to suppose, as many writers have done, that with the increasing dominance of scientific and rational thought, religion is on the way out for good. To argue in these terms is to ignore the fact that the very non-rational character of religion performs psychological and social functions, which cannot therefore be overcome by the substitution of scientific explanations of the universe.

Britain is now described as a Welfare State, a term whose relevance for religion is determined by the fact that the individual is now brought into contact with the Church less frequently. The typical crisis periods of life—birth, marriage and death—are less significant from the religious point of view because the State now interferes so much in them. Moreover, care of the poor and the sick is also undertaken primarily by State services. In the United States, on the other hand, the prevailing political philosophy has not permitted social welfare to proceed to a comparable stage, and this suggests a possible, but only partial, explanation of the greater importance of organized religion in that country. The Church has retained many of its social functions, and American priests are valuable social workers. Naturally, ordinary people who interact with the priests (while the latter are performing in their social-work capacity) develop sentiments which may well possess a religious content.

A number of significant studies can throw some light on the extent to which religious beliefs do exert control over people's thoughts and behaviour. Detailed examination of a rural village in Cumberland,* for example, revealed a marked apathy towards the Church which was by no means a recent phenomenon, although the blame was consistently placed on the shoulders of the new rector. Religious rites accompanying birth, marriage and death were regarded as merely

* Williams, W. M., *Gosforth*, Routledge & Kegan Paul, London, 1956.

signifying some change in status, although Confirmation was definitely viewed as a change in religious status alone. Indeed, Confirmation marked the climax of the most intensive period of church-going and religious instruction which was ever experienced during the whole life-time. It is interesting to note, in passing, that because of physiological and psychological changes, adolescence is the peak period for religious conversion, although such conversion may not be permanent. In Gosforth (the village concerned), the festivals with highest Church attendances were also those which were secular holidays. The general conclusion reached by the inquiry was that religion only exercised a very weak influence over the behaviour and mores of the community as a whole.

In the Swansea area of south-west Wales, there had been a decline in the impact of religion since World War I, but it was still a very real social force. Nearly half the population were church or chapel members, mainly the latter, and religious leadership was significantly linked with local government, political and trade union leadership. But because congregations were socially mixed, considerations of unity prevented individuals from discussing or determining social policy. The main factors in the decline of religious life were thought to be the growth of secular education and an increasingly materialistic interpretation of life, the democratic structure of chapel constitutions, and the influence of the Labour Party. The continuing strength of religion in this area, however, could be attributed chiefly to historical and cultural factors. This is borne out eloquently by the study of a semi-suburban London borough. Here only one-tenth of the population were at all closely associated with any of the churches, while at the other end of the scale, about two-thirds never, or practically never, went to church. However, the majority (80 per cent of the women and 65 per cent of the men) expressed a vague belief in God. The remainder felt a doubt rather than an active scepticism, and uncompromising disbelievers amounted to only 5 per cent of the total. Of the Church of England church-goers, under a third assented to the three basic tenets of the Creed, and 40 per cent doubted the possibility of an after-life. To most people, religion had come to mean little more than being kind and neighbourly, doing good when the opportunity arose. J. M. Mogey's study* of Oxford, too, revealed a very low frequency of church attendance. In Barton (the new housing estate) this could be partly accounted for by the absence of a proper church—a wooden hut was not accepted as a satisfactory substitute. A significant number of people both in Barton and in St. Ebbe's (the older residential area) explained that church-going was for children and youths, not for them. Some men even regarded attendance at religious services as a feminine practice.

Evidence to support the figures obtained in the London borough survey may be derived from the 1957 Gallup Poll on the subject, according to which only 6 per cent of Britain's population is atheist and only 16 per cent agnostic. These figures suggest that there has been no evident decline in beliefs about God, but rather an increasing apathy towards institutionalized religion. Further data showed that of the 78 per cent of the population believing in God, only 11 per cent of men and 16 per cent of women go to church. It is interesting to compare church membership (details of which are given in Table 21) with actual church attendance.

TABLE 21

Denomination	Membership (percentage of the total number of people of all denominations interviewed)
Church of England	55
Free Churches	15
Roman Catholic Church	9
Church of Scotland	7
Others	5
None	9
Total	100

Only 9 per cent of those claiming affiliation to the Church of England actually attended religious services, by contrast with 20 per cent of

* Mogey, J. M., *Family and Neighbourhood,* Oxford University Press, 1956.

the Free Church membership and 44 per cent of the Catholics. As regards the proportion of the total population which attends church, the Gallup Poll indicated that those who attend religious services once a month or more (including 13 per cent who attend once weekly at least) total 26 per cent of the total population. A similar number never goes to church at all. Age differences within the figures for church attendance suggest that older people predominate in congregations. This may be partly attributable to the fact that when people become older they begin to consider more seriously the implications of death, and also to the fact that older people may have fewer social or familial connections to keep them away from church (this is especially true if they have retired from active work). Cauter and Downham's inquiry into the leisure activities of Derby* found a close correlation between the figures for church attendance and cinema-going, at least for older people, although the figures for cinema-going were consistently the higher of the two. Finally, it was discovered that almost two-thirds of the total population had apparently never read the Bible and had not listened to any religious services on the radio during the 7 days previous to the inquiry. In answer to the question "Has religion more or less influence on your life than politics?" 41 per cent voted in favour of politics and only 30 per cent admitted the dominating importance of religion.

For young people, it is apparent that the under-20 age group shows significantly less religious conviction than other age groups. Whereas 78 per cent of the over-20 group believes in a God, this applies to only 62 per cent of the under-twenties. A recent survey by two social psychologists† has uncovered some interesting and possibly important trends in religious attitudes among undergraduates. On the basis of an attitude scale—from 40 for the strongly anti-religious to 136 for the very pro-religious—applied to a representative sample of students from all years and faculties, it was found initially that their general beliefs were predictable. A large minority (22 per cent) of extremely

* Cauter, T., and Downham, J. S., *Communication of Ideas*, Chatto & Windus, London, 1954.

† Pilkington, G. W., and Poppleton, P., both of the University of Sheffield; reported in the *Sunday Times*, 31 March 1963.

active, very religious students with a mean score of 116 was counterbalanced by a similar minority of very anti-religious students, atheists and agnostics, with a mean score of 60. In the middle was a solid group with mixed feelings of belief and doubt. The most striking discoveries were made when the psychologists went into detail, comparing the attitudes of the undergraduates with their chosen subjects of study. Arts students, for example, were obviously less religious by their second year at university than they were when they first came up, but the decline was reversed in later years and arts students often became the most intensively religious of all. With science students, on the other hand, the decline, apparent even in the first year, continued with each successive year at university. The psychologists reported that "the much popularized science versus religion conflict is still a real one for many science students". This is, in fact, a complete reversal of the positions of the two groups at the time of entry to university. Then it was the scientists who were most strongly religious, followed by the arts students. At all times, the highest pro-religious scorers were medical students in their final years and students training for teaching. However, the main purpose of the survey was to try to establish if there were signs of a religious revival. The psychologists concluded that the scores would need to be "much higher" before it could be claimed that religion is generally important to students. Only 23 per cent attended church once a week and only 16 per cent were members of university religious groups. But, for all that, no less than 63 per cent of the students held beliefs strong enough to make them say "private prayers."

Turning now to class differences in religious affiliations, the available evidence suggests that the working class is less active in this sphere, particularly as regards frequency of church attendance. This conclusion is supported by the 1957 Gallup Poll, whose figures showed that while 30 per cent of non-manual workers attended religious services once a month or more, the comparable figure for manual workers was only 17 per cent. Both the Gallup Poll and the Derby survey indicated a correlation between educational attainment and religious inclination. Nearly half of those who had received further education went to church once a month or more; by contrast, less than a quarter of those with only elementary education attended church. To a large extent, these figures can be interpreted as part of the class dichotomy, since those with more education are generally middle class in terms of occupation, style of life, manners, etc. Booth and other observers at the turn of the century had described the upper and middle classes as more active in religion, and he also referred to an "estrangement of the working classes", but whether this has continued it is impossible to say. Certainly Gorer discovered a tendency for people earning less than £5 a week to be more religious.

Between denominations, there is a slight likelihood that more members of the middle and upper classes belong to the Church of England, rather than to Catholic or non-conformist churches. In the U.S.A., Jews belong generally to a social class above that of Protestants, with the latter ranking higher than Catholics. Michael Argyle* says that social class influences religion rather than vice versa. The low position of Catholics may be partly due to the small incentive to achieve status which is characteristic of Catholicism and to the customarily low occupational status of many Catholic immigrants. Moreover, it is possible that the thrift encouraged by Protestantism results in social mobility, as suggested by Weber. According to Niebuhr,† all churches reflect the interests of the social class of the majority of their members. Thus it could be argued that the American liberal Protestant churches personify the political conservatism, nationalism, optimism and acceptance of the *status quo* which are characteristic of the upper middle class. Similar conclusions in this country may be drawn from Bottomore's study‡ of "Squirebridge". Among those inhabitants who were at all religiously inclined, the church was regarded as an association with specific aims, to which a definite amount of leisure time is devoted and which interferes little with other activities. Church of England affiliation involved a

* Argyle, M., *Religious Behaviour*, Routledge & Kegan Paul, London, 1958.

† Quoted in Argyle, M., *op. cit.*

‡ Bottomore, T., "Social Stratification in Voluntary Organizations", in Glass, D. V. (ed.), *Social Mobility in Britain*, Routledge & Kegan Paul, London, 1954.

relatively higher proportion of individuals from status groups A and B (in a three-category classification). The type of membership could, to some extent, be deduced from the style of life of the ministers. Those of the Church of England lived in fairly large houses (which they could no longer afford), while other ministers had fairly small homes. It was normal for leadership in church affairs to be assumed by those with higher occupational status, although social distinctions between the churches were declining in the face of a tendency for the squirearchy to be replaced by tradesmen and professional men in church organization.

Some writers have tried to show a distinction in the degree of religious attachment to be found in urban and rural areas. Gorer,* for example, found considerably more activity centred round the church in rural areas, and similar observations have been made in the U.S.A. If expressed on a graph, there would be a linear relation between religious activity and the size of the community, high for thinly populated rural areas and low for urban concentrations. One possible explanation for this is based on historical development: the greater activity in English rural areas and small towns could be due to cultural lag—large towns, as in other things, taking a lead in the decline of religion.

It has been suggested that religion prospers during periods of economic depression, but there is virtually no relationship between *per capita* incomes (at constant prices) and membership statistics for various churches. In Britain there has been an overall increase in prosperity since 1925, accompanied by a decline in religion. Although some religious leaders welcomed the depression because they felt people would return to the churches, in fact there was only a slight increase in affiliation to the Church of England and the Catholic Church, and none at all to the non-conformist bodies. In the U.S.A., by contrast, rising prosperity has been associated with increasing popularity for religion, particularly during the post-1945 economic boom, for all denominations and sects.

Urban communities, because of their large population, are able to support religious sects of various kinds, often originating as protest

* Gorer, G., quoted in Argyle, M., *op. cit.*

groups. In Britain, the smaller sects, like the Elim Foursquare Gospel Movement and the Jehovah's Witnesses, have not increased their overall membership since 1900. They may even be declining in much the same way as small political groups which can never establish themselves firmly in the face of competition from a few very large political parties. A contributing factor to the decline may be that the sects are largely comprised of poor people. As poverty declines the values of the sect itself have to maintain its cohesion against the world, without the supporting cohesion provided by common poverty.

The influence of religion changes in character, as society changes. As society develops from the simple to the complex, from the preliterate to the industrialized, so religion becomes delocalized, less anthropomorphic, more separated from everyday affairs. In the primitive village, religion seems to permeate every act, whereas in the modern city it is withdrawn into a separate category. Religious homogeneity tends to diminish, and there is increasing fragmentation of sentiments and ceremonies with the growth of the Church–State dichotomy. However, although the process of secularization can go a long way, there is an ultimate limit beyond which it cannot proceed, since a secular state can never perform the same cohesive function of religion.

Suggestions for Further Reading

General

CARR-SAUNDERS, A. M., CARADOG JONES, D., and MOSER, C. A., *A Survey of Social Conditions in England and Wales*, Oxford University Press, 1958.

GORER, G., *Exploring English Character*, Cresset Press, London, 1955.

CENTRAL OFFICE OF INFORMATION, *Britain: An Official Handbook*, H.M.S.O., London, Yearly.

Chapter 1

BANKS, J. A., *Prosperity and Parenthood*, Routledge & Kegan Paul, London, 1954.

GLASS, D. V., and GREBENIK, E., *The Trend and Pattern of Fertility in Great Britain, A Report on the Family Census of 1946*, H.M.S.O., London, 1954.

TOWNSEND, P., *The Last Refuge*, Routledge & Kegan Paul, London, 1962.

GENERAL REGISTER OFFICE, *Statistical Review of England and Wales*, Part 3, *Commentary*, H.M.S.O., London, Yearly.

Chapter 2

FLETCHER, R., *The Family and Marriage*, Penguin Books, 1962.

MCGREGOR, O. R., *Divorce in England*, Heinemann, London, 1957.

YOUNG, M. D., and WILLMOTT, P., *Family and Kinship in East London*, Routledge & Kegan Paul, London, 1957.

Chapter 3

COLE, G. D. H., *Studies in Class Structure*, Routledge & Kegan Paul, London, 1961.

GLASS, D. V. (ed.), *Social Mobility in Britain*, Routledge & Kegan Paul, London, 1954.

LOCKWOOD, D., *The Blackcoated Worker*, Allen & Unwin, London, 1958.

TITMUSS, R. M., *Income Distribution and Social Change*, Allen & Unwin, London, 1962.

ZWEIG, F., *The Worker in an Affluent Society*, Heinemann, London, 1961.

Chapter 4

BANKS, O., *Parity and Prestige in English Secondary Education*, Routledge & Kegan Paul, London, 1955.

DOUGLAS, J. W. B., *The Home and The School*, MacGibbon & Kee, London, 1964.

The Crowther Report (Report of the Central Advisory Council for Education —England), 15–18, H.M.S.O., London, 1959.

The Newsom Report (Report of the Central Advisory Council for Education —England), *Half our Future*, H.M.S.O., London, 1963.

The Robbins Report (Report of the Committee on Higher Education), *Higher Education*, H.M.S.O., London, 1963.

Chapter 5

HIMMELWEIT, H., OPPENHEIM, A., and VINCE, P., *Television and the Child*, Oxford University Press, 1958.

HOGGART, R., *The Uses of Literacy*, Chatto & Windus, London, 1957.

WILLIAMS, F., *Dangerous Estate. The Anatomy of Newspapers*, Longmans, London, 1957.

Chapter 6

BENNEY, M. *et al.*, *How People Vote*, Routledge, London, 1956.

GUTTSMAN, W. L., *The British Political Élite*, MacGibbon & Kee, London, 1963.

MCKENZIE, R. T., *British Political Parties*, Heinemann, London, 1955.

Chapter 7

ARGYLE, M., *Religious Behaviour*, Routledge & Kegan Paul, London, 1961.

WICKHAM, E. R., *Church and People in an Industrial City*, Lutterworth, London, 1957.

WILSON, B., *Sects and Society*, Heinemann, London, 1961.

Index

ASPECTS OF BRITISH POLITICS 1904-1919

DOREEN COLLINS,

Department of Social Studies, University of Leeds.

The intention of this book is to show the varied reactions to the changes in British foreign policy made necessary by the relative loss of British power at the beginning of the twentieth century and the subsequent diminution of confidence in the handling of foreign affairs. The effect of war on the nature of foreign affairs and on the traditional machine for the execution of foreign policy, which resulted in a sense of uncertainty and loss of morale within the Foreign Service, is elaborated by the author. She then indicates that at the end ofthe 1914-1918 war there was a demand for a reformed Foreign Service with an enlightened and democratic attitude to policy making. The book ends with a description of the aforementioned demands and the hopes and aspirations of a democratic foreign policy. This book will be of interest to all who wish to know more of this significant period of British History such as students at schools, technical colleges and universities.

BRITISH TRADE UNIONS TODAY

CLIVE JENKINS and J. E. MORTIMER

The book forms a good basis for the study of Trade Unions, covering the origin, growth, development, procedures, achievements and aims of the Trade Unions. It considers also their problems, and their future and while fully informative it is yet not too detailed to meet the needs of a wide readership.

The authors explain why more than one-sixth of the people of the British nation hold a trade-union membership card, what it involves, what they expect from their unions and how the trade-union movement affects their fellow citizens. Described also is the way in which the trade-union movement operates and how it strives constantly to achieve its objectives.

The authors are full-time trade-union officials and this account derives from their personal experience and close observation. Both have been involved in the basic organisation of workers and both have also taken part in political work to help obtain general social gains not obtainable by narrow industrial action. The unions themselves rest on the well-tried and valid concept that no man can or should reasonably seek to stand alone in matters of common concern.